FIRE
IN THE
JOHN

FIRE
IN THE
JOHN

By Alfred Gingold

CADER BOOKS

St. Martin's Press   New York

Produced by Cader Books
24 W. 10 Street
New York, NY 10011

Library of Congress Cataloguing-in-Publication Data

Gingold, Alfred.
    Fire in the john / Alfred Gingold.
        p.   cm.
    ISBN: 0-312-07483-2
    1. Machismo—Humor. 2. American wit and humor.   I. Title
    PN6231.M15G56 1991
    818' .5407—dc20   91–32824

A Thomas Dunne Book

10 9 8 7 6 5 4 3 2

This book is for Toby.

Acknowledgments

Heartfelt thanks to John Buskin and Judith Gingold for schmoozing under pressure; to Michael Carlisle and Cathy Plummer for service above and beyond the call; and most of all to Helen Rogan, for her indispensable advice, encouragement and affection.

— A. G.

Contents

FIRE
IN THE
JOHN

..
In
tro
duc
tion

A WAIL IN THE WILDERNESS

• •

Somewhere a man is *really getting into* changing his child's diaper.

Somewhere a man attends a dance recital in which no family members appear.

Somewhere a man lunches on pasta primavera.

Somewhere a man watches *Casablanca* and wonders how many Chesterfields would make him throw up.

What is the matter with these men?

They have lost their sense of what it means to be manly. Distracted, bereft of moral clarity, consumed with impossible ambitions (such as owning a Mercedes that is somehow not a German car) and unworkable passions (often a thing for Susan Dey), these men try to fill the chasm that yawns within with money, lust, drugs, drink, or property. To reclaim their youth, they take up roller-blading or aerobic dancing; they look ridiculous and they hurt themselves, but they plunge on. Bored with their dull suits and their functional leisure wear, they subscribe to magazines that promise knowledge of the perfect blazer and grow ponytails that everyone laughs at except other men with ponytails. They are too glazed to notice. They try Prozac, but it doesn't work. Nothing works.

All right, maybe they have a little fun for a while but eventually, the guy who knows not what a man is is an unhappy guy, whether or not he knows it. That's one thing we men know, somehow. Call them irresponsible, call them unreliable too, but men in ever-increasing numbers are looking at their lives, scratching their heads, and reaching for the Brioschi. What happened? Where have you gone, Joe DiMaggio?

He has lost his way.

Today's male is a confused, pathetic creature. He barely knows his wife or his children. He shares more with his colleagues at work, but he does not love them. In fact, he dreams of peeing in the punch bowl at the next Christmas party. He feels no satisfaction at having reached the fullness of maturity. Does he anticipate a graceful old age, revered as an elder in the bosom of his family? Ha. If he's lucky he looks forward to a condo in some obscenely sunny place, where the restaurants feature low-sodium specials and where he'll dress like a golfer for the rest of his days. His wife will probably survive him and invest the sweat of his brow in sun block and jewelry. He is an endangered species, with no

An old Nantucket "Chowder Man" treats alienated whalers with soup, c. 1848.

memory of steadfast manhood in his own experience and no living model to turn to. He is almost without hope.

Almost.

In ever-increasing numbers, men are waking up to their sense of loss and sharing it with anyone they can grab hold of. "The only time I know I'm a man is when I go to the little boy's room and see for myself," an anguished participant at my July Fourth "Foundering Fathers" Sweat Lodge Clambake shared with me once. "Now when I see what's doing Down There, I pretend it's a big flame-thrower, like the one Sly Stallone had in *Rambo II* and I'm running around shouting, hey guys, wake up! There's a fire. Fire in the john! Then I clean up around the bowl, flush and wash my hands."

This book joins him in that cry. Cleanup is his problem.

PART I

Hard Times for Soft Men

ORIGINS OF THE DEBACLE

• •

WHEN A MAN CLUBS A WOMAN— HUNTERS AND GATHERERS

How did a once-proud, some would say supercilious, gender reach this sorry state? Blame it on happenstance, double hammer-blows to exactly the same spot on the anvil of HIStory: the Industrial Revolution and the women's movement, two cataclysmic historical-tragical-pastoral events separated by little more than two World Wars, the Depression, the setting of the sun over the British Empire, Freud, Einstein and Elvis. This double-barreled trauma robbed the manchild of his birthright.

Gone forever are the days of the happy hunter-gatherer and spunky subsistence farmer. These hearty, hairy *patres familias* showed their sons how to bait traps and gut fish, how to distinguish poisonous berries from goat pellets—the corpus of mythic truths that have passed from father to son for eons, even when the little bastard doesn't deserve it.

The family unit as we know it did not exist before the invention of the station wagon. Prehistoric social units were large, the better to pursue big animals. Groups of nine or more formed softball teams to stay in shape when game was scarce. Intercave leagues were the first opportunity women had to throw like girls and get annoyed because the men took such a dumb pasttime so seriously. The seeds of bitter gender-resentment were sown.

These unpretentious primates, who roamed the earth goosing mastodons for fun, didn't need Wheaties to feel their oats. "How would you like a knuckle sandwich?" goes a vernacular greeting of the Pleistocene epoch, after which the neighbors/combatants (in Cavespeak they are the same word; see chart) would fall upon the ground and pummel each other until someone broke a limb. Then they would hobble away, dusty and blood-spattered, perhaps, but secure in the knowledge that each was a rootin'-tootin', honest-to-Jahweh man.

Notes on Cavespeak

Cavespeak is the earliest- known tongue that contains a word for "jock itch," but that is not the only reason it

Modern English	Cavespeak
Greetings	Banzai
Living-room set	Chattel
Wife	Chattel
Child	Chattel
Chattel	Say what?
Boss	Man with Big Pants
Mother Nature	The Little Woman
Bosom	Chest hair substitute
Honeymoon	The Hour of Defilement
Laundry	Woman's work
Bowling	Man's work

Fire in the John

is of interest to scholars of the masculine. No primitive patois more clearly suggests the patriarchal structure of early societies. Life was simple for these early humans. From dawn to dusk they ran around looking for food. If they couldn't hunt something down, they gathered something else up, and vice versa.

Hunting down huge carnivorous animals is not easy, and its requirements set the standards for male behavior that endure today: strength and silence. Women escaped this cruel soul distortion by going in for gathering, an inclination we see today in their love of shopping and ability to maximize limited closet space. Prehistoric men preferred to hunt despite its dangers because prehistoric gathered food was mostly twigs, dead grass, and bits of dirt.

Early females did not mind the gathered diet, even as today a man is likely to choose a cheeseburger over a spinach salad while a woman not only prefers the salad, she will remove the bacon bits from it and put them in your butter dish. The first vegetarians were women who noticed that leaves were easier to kill than beasts and contained less cholesterol as well:

Hunter-Gathering Man: (IN A WHISPER, EYEING STEGOSAURUS): Mmmmmm, pot roast for supper.
Hunter-Gathering Woman: Look, arugula! I've been looking all over for this. (BEGINS TO EAT BUSH MAN IS HIDING IN)
Hunter-Gathering Man: Stop that's my cover, you're eating my . . . Aaaargh! (IS TRAMPLED BY CHARGING STEGOSAURUS)
Hunter-Gathering Woman: (STEPPING AWAY, MUNCHING) Shhh. He'll hear you.

There was no sexual distinction between prehistoric genders during daylight hours. At night, something must have happened since—well, here we are. Eventually, astute males must have noticed that only the smaller hunter-gatherers bore children, while only the larger ones looked sheepish in the morning. Thus the family came into being, built on the triple pillars of guilt, mystification, and lust.

The first families changed life little. Children did not go to school. There were no schools. There was no need for any. There were no textbooks, no chalk, and hardly anything to learn. Early man was dumb as a post.

A hunter-gatherer mistakes branch of tree for wife.

Fire in the John

But his way of life was not without its merits. Father and son were together all day, every day. When they were not repairing arrowheads together, they were raiding someone else's pemmican depot. Competition was unknown, apart from softball. Relationships were forged in the fire of necessity. The word *friend*, in fact, means "he who keeps you from being gored." In this way, boys learned to become men—the ones that made it.

For many died young and violently. Life was poor, nasty, brutish, and short—just like early man, actually. Age was a badge of honor. To live long was a tribute to strength and intelligence. The Indo-European root of "old" also means "smart cookie," while the root of "youth" means "Wait a while, big shot."

The psyches of these primitive men were ruled by what we call the "Wild Man" archetype, (see p. 35), only now he is called the "Vile Man" because of the hunter-gatherer's terrible manners. He ate with his hands; his nose ran and his feet smelled, prompting some to presume that he was upside down, but he simply didn't know any better. Only when he began to farm did he calm down.

THE SILENCE OF THE YAMS

As early man settled down and planted crops, the blood lust that the hunt satisfied did not go away. The first farmers were just as fierce as their hunting forebears. Indeed, most of them would have preferred hunting for bears, but they had responsibilities to family, as their wives (Mithraic for "little nudzh") pointed out. Our ancestors did the right thing; the Wild Man became a utility fielder.

Agrarian societies are not noted for their clever conversationalists, and the earliest human settlements were no exception. Cultivating crops with crude implements such as sticks and teeth left little time to cultivate the spirit. Few early men even knew they had spirits. If they opened their mouths it was usually to eat or scream with horror.

At day's end, families sat around campfires singing folk songs. Fathers and mothers would teach their offspring the harmony parts for "Michael, Row Your Boat Ashore." Agrarian man lived in rare harmony with his world. It was a quiet time for civilization and it lasted for thousands of years, interrupted only by occasional outbreaks of pestilence, religious mania or inexplicable warfare.

ENGINES OF ENTERPRISE

Man's drowsy idle was disrupted forever by the clatter of the nineteenth century. The Machine Age and the Industrial Revolution took off simultaneously. What a racket! Men put down their hoes, said good-bye to their families and marched off to factories. There they contracted black lung, hemorrhoids, flat feet, chronic hearing loss, and carpal tunnel syndrome.

Fathers became elusive strangers, lurching exhausted and preoccupied through their sons' lives. There is nothing like factory labor to bring out man's Inner Zombie.

Man was deprived of more than his health and his quality time. He was robbed of his self-esteem, too. A farmer who grows a tomato has brought life out of the earth, life that needs only a little oil, vinegar and

Who knows what this thing does? Not the people who operate it.

seasonings to make a tasty first course all by itself. A hired hand who tightens a screw on a widget or heaves a bale of cotton into the gin (onto the gin? around the gin? who can truly say?) feels no comparable pride. He doesn't own what he's made. He may not even know what the hell it is, much less get any pleasure from it. Instead, he takes his money home and, along the way, stops for a little drinky-poo.

Meanwhile, who's tending the home fires? Guess.

Now the son learns about manhood not from the father, but from the mother, who's peeved after millennia of gathering followed by centuries of housework. Maybe it was asking too much of her to refrain from poisoning the children with her resentment, but the loss of good old pre-industrial Dad has never been properly recognized, let alone mourned.

There has been no time to mourn. Scarcely one hundred sixty years after mechanization signaled the end of the happy times, women administered their blow to male stature: they went toe to toe with men in the workplace and did just fine.

The Fair Sex Cries Foul

While man's spiritual back was being broken, woman continued to voice her concerns to her children, her friends, even the barnyard animals. Unlike man, who had to shut up to survive, woman did not neglect the need to reflect on life and grumble about it robustly. The therapeutic benefits of complaint are reflected in the very word "woman," a corruption of "woe-man," Old Norse for "the shapely one who does not clam up" and the Wisconsin dialect variant, "Whoa-man," an untranslatable idiom which means something like, "Lucky for you cheesemakers are nonaggressive."

Women have never lost touch with their expressive power. Theirs is a lesson we men would do well to learn. Most men are simply incapable of, say, bursting into tears in the kitchen, even if their wives have been making them chop the onions since day one of the marriage. Who can argue with them? No wonder women have controlled our homes for decades.

You'd think that would keep them happy, wouldn't you?

Now, no one begrudges women the fantastic clout they've amassed in the world less than we New Men do. We're glad women have moved into the work force with the zeal of Genghis Khan. We welcome the ladies into the "real" world and we wish them God's speed. If you'd given us a little warning, we would have whipped up a get-acquainted ritual. Now we can turn our attention inward, to what's left of our souls, and outward, to a world we never made. Something is very wrong in both places.

The Wild Man has disappeared from our souls and from our behavior. He has been replaced by the Mild Man. The Mild Man doesn't run around our psyches littering and cursing and clamoring for excitement. He might jog and hum along with his Walkman, but no more than two or three times a week. The Mild Man doesn't get excited. He takes things seriously, but not to the point of missing a workout. Ugh.

Mild at Heart: Kevin Costner, a Robin Hood who doesn't have all the answers.

Errol Flynn doesn't know there are any questions, but is man enough to wear green tights.

Our movie stars are mild. Our cars have lost their fins. Men eat too many turkey sandwiches and not enough steak tartare. Type A behavior, which used to be called Good Old American Get Up and Go, is frowned upon. And with good reason, too, because that stuff'll kill you. And yet (stay calm as you read this if you can): Women get to wear shoulder pads the size of a Green Bay Packer's and butt heads in the business world like they own the joint.

This is progress.

MYTHING IN
ACTION

$\bullet\bullet$

Any man who feels himself at a loss today must look with envy at the prehistoric family. What did those fathers know, he asks, that his modern descendants do not? What must those rudimentary men have been like?

Hicks, really, tight-lipped, horny-handed sons of the soil with no interests and no time for any anyway. Not a one of them had so much as a high school education. What the hell did they have to teach?

They had myth, that's what. The power of myth kept them on course. And myth is what we lack today.

Life wasn't a bowl of nuts and berries for primitive

Cave dweller attempts to shoot craps,
not knowing dice shouldn't be round
and you need two.

man. Evidence suggests that some prehistoric men dealt with pressure just as their progeny do today. Among artifacts found near the cave paintings at Lascaux was a crudely fashioned television remote. Thousands of years ago, a wiped-out hunter-gatherer avoided his family by staring at the wall. Eventually, he got fed up with the dancing cows and tried to find ESPN.

WHAT IS MYTH?

A *myth* is a story so deeply rooted in the heart of the culture from which it springs that no royalty or trademark agreements impinge upon it. Scholars, troubadours and poets may quote, paraphrase, and pilfer myths without fear of legal action. Sometimes they try to create new myths, usually in connection with weekend seminars. This is called *mythopoeic* activity because it is more fun to say than *mythic*, even though no one is quite sure how to pronounce it. Modern stories sometimes become myths too, like "The Honeymooners" and "All in the Family," but usually only after they've gone into syndication.

HOW DO MYTHS WORK?

Myths teach us how to get through the crucial moments of life. When they cease to help us, myths lose their potency, which is why practicing tree-worshipers are so hard to come by. What, after all, do trees know?

The most significant passages in life are birth, coming of age, marriage, and death. Some people would rank having children and buying a first home equal to the first four, but there is no myth that tells us how to behave at a closing. Just bring lots of Dramamine.

The myths we are interested in are those that tell boys how to become men. These are *myths of initiation*. They exist in many cultures and usually involve enough spears, tunnels, deep lakes, and wounds to make a Freudian wet his pants.

There are far fewer female initiation myths. Women don't need them as much because they *menstruate*, Nature's loudest wake-up call. Consequently, girls reach maturity without having to read any more on the subject than *Heidi* or *Marjorie Morningstar*.

Male initiation myths are terribly complicated, because men are so complicated. Myths are necessary to teach boys how to acknowledge the various aspects of male identity and reconcile their warring needs, if only so he can get out the door in the morning. Before he can control his identity, he must first understand it.

FOREVER JUNG:
A GUIDE TO MALE ARCHETYPES

Man's spiritual nature is multifaceted. Inside each of us is a sick man and a well man, a strong and a weak, an inner child and an inner adult, someone who does an excellent impression of Ida Lupino and another who wears a chicken suit. The guy in the chicken suit is the Trickster.

There is a Trickster in every mythology in the world. In the Norse legends he is Skeggi the Irascible Travel Agent, who books other gods on package tours to Greenland in the middle of winter when the place is deader than a doornail. To the French he is Henri, the wily stoat of Alsace, who darts around the countryside magically changing the color of everybody's wine. The Lakota Sioux have Walks-Dorky, a laconic (even for them) brave who fakes war wounds so he can stay

Tricksters cavort at annual convention. Who knows where they got the drum?

behind and make merry with the squaws. From these tales we see that the capacity to be a dissembling, insufferable jerk is found in all men. There are other capacities men share:

Fire in the John

THE WILD MAN: Covered with unruly hair full of split ends, close to the earth, the Wild Man embodies anarchy, the atavistic, primitive core, the part that picks up chicken parts and eats with his fingers. Our society would like to eradicate this most endangered of interior mythic species.

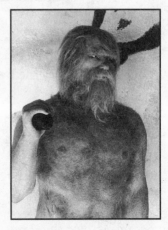

Last Book Read: *Chaos*.

Likes: Girls who like to dance, big portions, anything by the Stones.

Dislikes: People who are stuck-up, wire-rimmed glasses, Kleinian analysis.

Favorite Songs: "Almost Cut My Hair," "Woolly Bully."

Quote: "Toga, toga, toga."

THE TRUE KING: Leader, rational, thinking part of our nature. Designates goals, principles. Maintains standards inside psyche.

Last Book Read: Who's got time to read?

Likes: Clean sheets, Vivaldi, *Masterpiece Theatre*, all the Royals except Fergie.

Dislikes: troublemakers

(like some spirits I could name but won't), uncertainty, dull kitchen knives.

Favorite Movie: *The Lion in Winter*.

Favorite Songs: "Dang Me," "My Way."

Quote: "Uneasy lies the head that wears the crown."

THE LOVER: Romance and erotic feeling grow from the Lover. Modulating his urges and making sure they are not directed toward, say, an unsuspecting coat tree, are jobs for the other inner spirits. The Lover inside us would do it with a snake if he could get one to hold still. His loins percolate.

Last Book Read: *Listen to the Warm*.

Likes: What d'ya got? And, of course, Fred and Ginger.

Dislikes: Sexual repression, anything beige, the studio cut of *Heaven's Gate*.

Favorite Movies: *Swing Time*, *Love Story*, *Debbie Does Dallas*.

Favorite Songs: "Built for Comfort," "That's Amore."

Quote: "Would you like to see my etchings?"

THE WARRIOR: Protects boundaries of self, agent of will, heart and brain, in no particular order. "That's not for me to decide," says the Warrior, "I just follow orders." Poorly developed in modern man, the Inner Warrior prevents people from imposing on you, whether it be your wife or a total stranger who walks up to you and

jams a tongue depressor in your mouth, just for laughs.
Last Book Read: *The Peloponessian Wars* (but can't wait for the Schwarztkopf bio)
Likes: orienteering, thumb wrestling, Scrabble.

Dislikes: ballet, M.R.E.'s, any mind-altering substance stronger than iced tea.
Favorite Movie: *Apocalypse Now*.
Favorite Song: "The Caissons Go Rolling Along."
Quote: "Nuts."

THE CHILD: Every bit as uncivilized as the Wild Man, and not toilet trained to boot, the Inner Child is all appetite, driving even the Trickster crazy with his constant demands and mood swings. The most indulged of all the inner beings, some men let theirs out at parties.

Last Book Read: *The Runaway Bunny*.
Likes: sleeping, eating, pooping, strained apricots.
Dislikes: Daddy (you were expecting something different?), tight diapers, feeling excluded.
Favorite Movies: *Babysongs, 101 Dalmatians, Debbie Does Dallas*.
Quote: "More juice."

THE SHAMAN, or PRESS AGENT, a.k.a. "Bernie": The Inner Bernie knows how long each of the other inner beings should hold sway over you and how to manage your maturation career in general.

(Bernie hates to be photographed. He would rather emphasize his clients.)

Last Book Read: *Chutzpah.*
Likes: good people, promptness.
Dislikes: Shnorrers.
Quote: "I always take the long view. And a percentage of the gross."

THE SUFFERING MAN: This is the part of the soul for which every half-full glass is half-empty. The Suffering Man is able to bring those around him down into the black hole of his unhappiness. Society frowns on the Suffering Man. Even the other Inner Beings try to avoid him, pretending to read their papers when he comes by and moving to parts of the soul where they think he won't be. He's a downer.

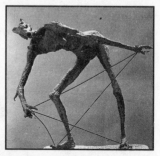

Last Book Read: *Despair,* and before that *Misery.*
Likes: Hard to say, I've got so many allergies.
Dislikes: Don't ask.
Favorite Movie: *Dark Victory* ("To me, it's funny.")
Favorite Song: "Nobody Knows You When You're down and Out."
Quote: "Who says white people can't have the blues?"

WHAT'S BUGGING OUR ARCHETYPES?

Our Inner Beings have not gone anywhere. They still live within us, doing the best they can. But they are starving. The old stories are no longer being told and the libraries do not stock them. In their place are new myths, myths that reflect our times (*see chart*), not the eternal verities of our soul-needs.

MODERN MYTHS
AND WHAT THEY TEACH

Myth	Teaching
Fatal Attraction	All quickies are nut jobs who will end up coming after you with a knife, so dress warmly and don't stay out late.
Field of Dreams	Clap your hands if you believe in the Black Sox and Dad will return from the dead.
Operation Desert Storm	A properly run war should take less time than the victory parade clean-up.
Two-Party Democracy	Voters have a choice.
TeenageMutant Ninja Turtles	Youthful enthusiasm is charming.
The Godfather, Part Three	There is no such thing as a dead horse.

Without the traditional tales, our Inner Kings have lost their way and can no longer lead. The Warrior skulks. He has become timid, allowing anyone who wants to invade our spiritual boundaries. He may be using steroids. The Warrior needs the King to slap his face and send him on a ten-mile hike with full pack.

The rest of the archetypes aren't any happier. There's talk of forming a union behind the king's back and striking for vacation pay and shorter hours. No one's got the nerve to approach the King, though.

Do not blame your inner archetypes for the myths they act in. Like any actors, they're only as good as the scripts they get. "Give me the right myth, I'll cheer up in a minute," says the Suffering Man. "As far as I'm concerned, Bernie isn't doing his job." Our myths are no help to him or us.

Irate archetypes meeting in secret.

THE WAY WE
LIVE NOW

• •

T he old disadvantages of manhood remain. We open the doors, die younger, go balder, compute the tip. We fight in wars and have to wear ties and jackets to restaurants even in summer. We knock ourselves out trying to find a video you can both stand to watch. Women, on the other hand, usually get custody and their choice of aisle or window seat. They can wear cute little outfits that laugh at the weather; try that if you're a guy in Duluth and your supervisor will break your legs in the night.

The new tribulations are what's breaking us. It's the new stuff. Others now demand the respect we once only had to accord to each other: women, minorities, pets— excuse me, animal companions. A man's got nowhere to turn if he needs to let off a little steam.

Not that there's much steam left. Newfangled creations like central air and the rule of law have weakened the species in the name of improving it. The depth of male unhappiness can no longer be disregarded. It goes without saying that the academic community has noticed.

THE SCHOLARS:
BREAKING WINDS OF CONTROVERSY
Professor Allen K'bloom, author of *The Closing of the American Blind*, investigates the disintegration of

American family life from his aerie high atop the University of Chicago's Institute of Portentous Studies. There, armed with a powerful telescope, he nightly peers into the windows of local homes. "The night is best for the work that I do," he says, "Because the night time is the right time to be with the one you love. Besides, if I got caught up here snooping during the daytime, it could cost me tenure, so who needs the agoravation? Get it? Agora-vation. It's *ancient Greek*, for Chrissake."

Professor K'bloom and acolytes proudly display their large heads.

K'bloom finds that today's family man looks out from behind his newspaper fifty percent less than he did ten years ago. He does not help his children with their homework and speaks to his wife only when the snack bowl needs refurbishment.

"It's not healthy, this lack of communication," K'bloom says candidly. "In the bedroom, well, I can't really say. Most people around here know about me and pull their curtains. The ones who don't . . . well, words fail me. And it's a good thing, too, because I'm facing an injunction. But speaking off the record, I say they've lost their Zeus Energy. It's a terrible thing to lose your Zeus energy."

THE WANE OF ZEUS ENERGY

Zeus energy is the spirit of male dominion and agency that has always allowed men to achieve, to conquer, to be fruitful and multiply, or just to have a nice piece of fruit if that's all he wants (see *The Fruits of Your Labors*, p. 51). Zeus energy enables man to follow the Firebird of his destiny as far as it will take him, even unto the Pontiac Dealership Eternal.

Zeus energy shows up in all mythologies and cultures, from the noblest to the most primitive. Graffiti in a prehistoric cave near Tyson's Corner Shopping Mall in Virginia depict a large, floppy-eared canine god figure who wreaks vengeance on the shoppers by lifting his leg, forming the headwaters of the Potomac and creating the swampy, fetid environment that makes politicians in nearby Washington, D.C., feel right at home. He is Phlegm, the Ur–doggie-mentor whose growling (thunder) lured the men of the tribe away from their shelters in hopes of secret teaching. When the men are isolated, alone, and afraid, Phlegm makes it "rain." Ha! The ancient gods were more than manly. They appreciated

Zeus and friend Tiffany at ease on Mount Olympus.

a good joke.

"We have no more doggy gods, no Phlegm, no Zeus," K'bloom laments. "I have a lot of pain about that." In the absence of the real thing, he argues, we've resorted to hybrids and synthetics:

Bruce Energy: Big box office, but softies at heart. Flannel shirts and chin bristles do not real men make.

Moose Energy: How many weights must a man lift up before you will call him a man? Enough is enough. In Germany, this syndrome is called *Shwarzeneggergnugen*.

Spruce Energy: Is dressing well the best revenge? He thinks so. His Rolex and custom suit are the feather headdresses and penis sheaths of our tribe. Behind his back, his wife cheats on him and his son imitates the way he sips his morning coffee—sorry, I mean decaf. His secretary calls him Sasquatch.

A DISSENTING VIEW

Camille Piglia , author of *This Little Piglia Went to Grad School* and *How to Make Love to a Semiotician* among others, is a real anomaly in the academic world. Not satisfied with a distinguished career as teacher and writer, she operates a traveling abattoir out of her minivan, slaughtering animals for local farmers, hunters, and the occasional, goaded-beyond-endurance pet-owner (Excuse me, that's goaded-beyond-endurance animal companion's human companion.)

Ms. Piglia with her dander up.

"The thirst for knowledge comes, it goes; the hunger for a nice piece of meat is eternal, I don't care what your blood levels are." She agrees with K'bloom that American men are less interested than ever in relationships.

"Let's face it, men stink, they always have, they always will," she says, "But nowadays, you have to set their hair on fire just to get 'em to say boo." Before she could elucidate, Miss Piglia excused herself to "put on her face." It was Hawaiian night at a local boîte, and she was "hoping to find a nice lei."

Ms. Piglia differs from K'bloom as to the source of the current malaise. In fact, their positions couldn't be more different. To quote Ms. Piglia, "Did K'bloom start that Zeus crap? What a load of bull pookie."

Ms. Piglia sees the mythic roots of the calamity closer to home, in the demise of John Wayne, whose real first name, Ms. Piglia cannot stop reminding us, was Marion. As she says, "His real first name was Marion."

Incredible but true: His real first name was Marion.

THE WANE OF WAYNE

When John Wayne strode off into that gilded twilight that is reserved for ancient Republican actors, he took with him a conception of American manhood to which many aspired: man as inanimate object. Blame it on the sixties, blame it on Vietnam, or blame it on all those boring evenings that women and children have passed while dad sits rippling his jaw muscles and hogging the dip, solid as a rock, and just as much fun. No one's been able to pull off the rock act quite like Wayne.

We have much to learn from the mineral world and indeed all inert material, but we know today that man, by his nature, aspires to erthood. It has been a long struggle to face this.

OF ROCKS AND MEN—A COMPARISON

Man	Rock
Capable of change	Only if you've got lots of time
May wince at sight of own blood	Feels no pain (and an island never cries)
Can tell waiter "No MSG, please"	Eats like a bird, even less
Must be forced onto dance floor	Won't dance, don't ask it
Deeply concerned with aging	Philosophical about place in cosmos. Likes to sit and smell the lichen, then poof! Country roads, take me home

My Brother Esau is an Hairy Man,
But I Have to Shave Every Goddamn Day

For many, the seed of the discontent lies in the workplace. Work is highly regarded today but remember, it was God's punishment to Adam and Eve for eating the apple and . . . well, you know what they did. They also gave up a very nice property with wildlife, fruit trees, and water frontage and had to get a whole new wardrobe. They had to go to work. What can we learn from this?

Work is not a virtue. Work is retribution—practically a sin, certainly an offense against nature. I feel this to be true. So do you. The cultures of antiquity understood this. Even primitive cultures—excuse me, I mean alternative–technologically–abled cultures—agree with this view.

In the language of the Kh'a-k'ha-pupu people of the South Pacific, for instance, the word for "job-holder" also means "one so impossibly stupid he couldn't find his ass with both hands." What do the Kh'a-k'ha-pupu know that we are afraid to admit? I'll tell you.

The Truth About Work

Work is boring. That's why nobody ever works in the movies. Oh, actors stride around with briefcases or wrenches looking purposeful, but invariably they're shot or in bed with someone before lunch. Hollywood knows that the proudest badge of adulthood our society offers, "enjoying your work," is nothing but a shield from spiritual emptiness, not to mention from our families. Despite labor-savers like computers, fax machines and microwaves, we work harder today than at any time in history. No wonder even our disks are floppy.

Why and how this occurred is a subject too depressing not to have its own little section (see next section). For now we need only realize that we live in the shadow of a vast conspiracy to make us think work is good for us. The agents of this conspiracy are powerful and many, including past and present bigwigs of industry, religion, and politics. People, in short, with a vested interest in your productivity, not your happiness. The name of this conspiracy is the Work Ethic or, as it is called in Eastern Europe, the *Work Shmethic*.

THE WORK SHMETHIC

When we identify ourselves by occupation, we are victims of the Work Shmethic. When the first words we hear at a party are "What do you do?" we are victims of the Work Shmethic. When you wish your competitor would contract a wasting disease and he's not really a bad guy, just sort of a jerk, you are a victim of the Work Shmethic. Too much Work Shmethic depletes the imagination, deprives us of insight and overview, and makes us too tired to think about having fun.

Look at the business page of the paper. You see a lot of pudgy men in over-priced suits and chauffeur driven limousines. These men control the world, making more money for bigger limousines to go in greater comfort to earlier graves.

No ancient Greek of means would knock himself out the way these jokers do. No, the ancient Greek would arise early to breathe in unpolluted Aegean air. He'd bathe, breakfast and, clad only in a simple tunic or *chiton*, spend a few hours in his garden, perchance, relaxing with a good scroll. He'd ponder the cosmos, feeling his chest fill with enough Zeus energy to blow the handles off an amphora at sixty feet. He would have lunch. Afterward he'd meander over to the Acropolis and check out the scene, perhaps chewing the fat with members of the Peripatetic School.

Sound like a good way to live? You bet it does. And it is. I spend as much time as I possibly can lounging in my *chiton*, pondering the cosmos, and preparing for lunch. It's not really a *chiton*, it's more of a terry cloth bathrobe, but I can pretend it's whatever I want it to be, because my imagination is not dead. I resist the Work Shmethic.

Etymological Note: The Fruits of Your Labors
It's no surprise that the reward of work is often referred to metaphorically as fruit, for those piquant offspring of the mature she-plant often pack an intestinal wallop. An ambitious or driven man is said to have a "fire in his belly." Many idioms for money and success involve indigestibility: potatoes (if fried), bananas (if too green or many), clams (in months without an R), chicken feed (if you're not a chicken), dough (if it hasn't risen).

What does this tell us? Simply that if you work too much, you may own many things. These possessions may be items of sophisticated design and elaborate manufacture, like stereo systems and precious jewelry. Elsewhere, these rewards will be more organic, but no less corrupting. In St. Lucia, to offer a gratuity is to "put a mango in [his] hat," with the clear implication that a hat can hold only so many mangoes. We must not be enslaved to the fruits of our labors. Too much fruit is not good for you. And when you eat fruit, be sure you wash it carefully first.

PARDON YOU FOR LIVING:
YOUR CHILDREN
In the good ur-days, a man could count on a modicum

of respect from his children. Your sperm, after all, have determined half their physiological makeup, and it stands to reason that something that grew from your own sperm would like you.

This is no longer true. Fertility labs across the country report cases of fast-moving bands of sperm, armed with tiny weapons, climbing up their donors' neckties and trying to strangle them. Even before your children

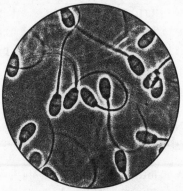

Here, recovering sociopathic sperm rehearse "Dance at the Gym" sequence from West Side Story.

are conceived, they do not like you. What have you done that's made the unborn irate?

Sperm are small, but they are not stupid. They know a plastic cup in a laboratory is not where they're supposed to be. Being flash frozen in a plastic bag is worse yet. These sperm know more than they want to know about the tremendous strides medicine has made in expanding the possibilities of conception. Suddenly, the poor sperm's role in the drama is reduced from star player to prop in an elaborate special-effects display, culminating in a frantic open-air swim across a petri dish, cheered on by technicians acting as if they were taking in the Oxford-Cambridge Boat Race.

Fire in the John

Sperm that are abused in this way have every right to be mad. Their defiant rage, before they've even met any eggs, must give pause to Pro-Choicers, especially those who believe that a fetus is not fully human until it can identify its favorite Beatle. (And it remains a fetus if its favorite is Paul.)

It's not all your fault, though. If your child is old enough for you to really grate on each other, it follows your sperm has met an egg. Your wife's egg. But it's still mostly your fault. Just ask your wife.

THE TIES THAT STRANGLE:
YOUR WIFE

Gerard Manly "Mary" Poppins, a marriage counselor whose office features the padded canvas floor of a boxing ring, often begins sessions with an arm wrestling match between the marriage partners. In over seventy percent of cases, the wife not only takes the husband two out of three, she then tries to break the son of a bitch's arm.

"These men and women are not getting along," "Mary" said to me last time we ran into each other in our bongo instructor's waiting room, "In fact, they hate each other's cotton-picking guts. You should hear the things they say to one another. I blush to think of them."

Small wonder. The last few decades have seen the old patterns collapse. Women have fought for, and won, a measure of respect that no one begrudges them less than I. Their needs are addressed by politicians and the media. Everyone's had to learn how to pronounce "Ms." It's gotten so a person can't turn on the television without finding out what "light days" are. Man is learning more than he ever thought he would about the oppression of women, often on the first date. Hell, they even let'em fly jets now. It's been great for the ladies, and no one is happier for them than I and all manly men.

But let's be fair.

Men have it coming at them from every direction. Technology makes us feel small, insignificant, puny. Our computers make us obsolete the minute we figure out how to turn the goddamn things on. Our sex drive is dampened by the knowledge that what is mid-life for the goose is way the hell past it for the gander. Even our winsomely appealing love of sport and male companionship is ridiculed. What is left for us?

Every culture but ours has elaborate legend systems about the group's sky parents, representing what is sacred and spiritual. They also have an earth mother and earth father, representing the factual and physical. Sky parents and earth parents bicker and part, make up and procreate, read the newspapers and take in the mail. They kiss your boo-boos. They attend celestial P.T.A. meetings and once in a while dine out together, nothing fancy. They embody marital harmony.

We have no such stories to tell ourselves. All we can do to fill the gap is eat a Sky Bar which is very nice, especially the nougat, but it isn't the same thing. Is it any wonder so many marriages founder? They have no maps, no traditions, and only one piece of nougat.

GROWING OLD DISGRACEFULLY

In Parisian subways there are seats reserved for the aged and infirm.

In Japan, Shintoists worship the spirits of their ancestors.

In Africa, elders become *griots*, repositories and transmitters of the tribal culture.

In America, senior citizens can get an early-bird dinner special at many coffee shops if they are willing to eat and get out before seven.

We do not respect the old the way others do. The elders of the Kh'a-k'ha-pupu are esteemed as their most beautiful citizens; indeed, the word for beautiful also means "as wizened as a neglected coconut."

The Kh'a-k'ha-pupu are scrotal fetishists. The tribe's hunters decorate themselves with talismans fashioned from the nether parts of male groundhogs and voles.

Senior citizens debate merits of their breakfast treats in effort to remain engagé.

The diminutive organs of these small mammals heighten the hunters' sense of empowerment. To them there is a natural connection between what is shrivelled and fuzzy and what is mature, full of wisdom, experience, seed. For the Kh'a-k'ha-pupu there are rewards to old age that go beyond free soup and salad.

Our own elderly are not nearly so fortunate. They know they are only a category in a quarterly report, of concern only to makers of ear hair–remover and rubber panties. Their children avoid them and their government chips away at their social security. So they fight aging with plastic surgery, trousers with just a scoche more room (What the hell is a scoche?) and more stimulating new interests than is healthy for anyone.

We owe the aged a more graceful declension. They are one oppressed people whose number we all hope to join. Besides, the words of the aged hold remarkably true. Yes, the world really has gone to hell in a handcart and today's young really are irretrievably snot-nosed and unappreciative. Who knows whose fault it is? MTV, probably, and the makers of all those sugary breakfast cereals, and fluoride, definitely fluoride.

Is this man to blame for the state of our young?

Sadly, disrespect for the old is the least of our problems.

Fire in the John

CROCK OF AGES

We find deep reservoirs of truth in the utterances of the old. Their banal drivel has for too long has been dismissed as the senile rumblings of old geezers waiting to die. Drivel like this:

- Things ain't what they used to be.
- Kids today get away with murder.
- As long as you've got your health.
- You can have wine after beer. Avoid beer after wine. [invalid if large quantities of chicken wings with blue cheese dressing are involved.]
- When you forget your umbrella, it rains.
- Finding a good parking spot can cure hay fever.

What simple wisdom these words hold, like the truths of Hansel and Gretel and the infield fly rule that all men know in their hearts.

Not that we should confuse every venerable folk inanity we hear with the truth. Here are some that aren't:

- It isn't the heat, it's the humidity. [It's the heat.]
- You can have white wine after red. Avoid red wine after white. [It's all fine.]
- It ain't the meat, it's the motion. [It's at least partly the meat. 35%–65% split, tops].
- Starve a cold, feed a fever. [Feed everything.]
- Life begins at forty. [Life insurance, maybe]

TIRED DOWN BELOW

Sexual dysfunction strikes earlier and with, um, withering ferocity. A new strain of impotence is upon the land. All over the world, men are not in the mood. The ancients were familiar with impotence. The Greek poet Pusillanimous revealed as much knowledge of the problem as any sex therapist:

> *When it won't stand up,*
> *There's just no stopping it.*

But that lyric was written for a man

> *So old he was like unto a cheese*
> *Forgotten in the larder 'til so moldy*
> *The smell of it made you gag.*

And afflicted with a wife who was

> *Beefier than a Rottweiler,*
> *Enough to make a man go "Whew!"*
> *And stay late at the taverna.*

An impotent ancient knew where to place the blame for his condition: elsewhere. The classic diagnosis, "It's not my fault," is typical of the Old Impotence. Today's impotent man finds in his predicament the source of yet more ancestral anguish, and at the same time, another experience to share.

Impotent ancient attempts to divert wife with Zorba impression.

Is the New Impotence a new sexual disorder related to the collapse of masculinity in our time? Can it explain the pathetic dearth of viable Democratic Presidential timber? Do our bodies know something we don't? Have our spongy cells Down There received a message that our heads and hearts are only now picking up? Just thinking about it makes me want to lie down with a cool compress over my eyes.

EXCUSES, EXCUSES

Old Impotence: Common Alibis
I had some bad shellfish.
This has never happened to me before. What
    about you?
It's your perfume.
You've gained weight.
You've lost weight.
I need to be wearing my chaps.

New Impotence: Common Alibis
I'm not in touch with my Wild Man.
I'm too much in touch with my Trickster.
I've never met my Warrior.
It's my Lover's night off.
All that salad doesn't agree with me.
I need to be wearing my chaps.

CAN WE SAVE OURSELVES?

• •

To sum up, today we are a gender devoid of heroes. The desire for an old-fashioned father is so great that for eight years we had a President with a pompadour, a hairstyle not seen for half a century. Our inadequacies have been illuminated for us from many different points. We have swallowed it all.

We suffer from PMSS: Post-Macho Stress and Strain. We're mad as hell about what's happened to us, but have no idea of what to do about it. We have lost touch with our fortitude, passion, grief. Some of us can't even find our car keys.

Gone into hibernation are the Wild Man, the Warrior, the King. Bernie's somewhere in the Caribbean, he wouldn't say where. Man has become an alienated Milquetoast, an allergy sufferer, a wimp, a dweeb. No wonder the Democrats can't find a decent candidate.

It's a good thing I got here when I did.

Take a deep breath and a drink of water, then settle down and do the following quiz. There are no right and wrong answers to it. That would be competitive, just what we're avoiding (see Step Two, p. 76). Not that I wouldn't know how to score it. I know what your answers mean. But don't worry about it. I'm not counting. Look at this simply as a way to see how much of a man you are. No fair comparing answers with other softies!

WHAT KIND OF FOOL ARE YOU?
(a quiz for men)

Note: This test is not restricted to men only. We recommend different hormonally-abled readers to take it as well.

1. *At a restaurant with your spouse or espousal equivalent, your waiter serves you an Amaretto sour by mistake. Should you:*

 a) Throw it at the bastard?

 b) Consume the entire drink, including the glass and swizzle stick?

 c) Send it back, insisting on your martini?

 d) Assume the waiter's got a lot on his mind, and go ahead with your meal?

2. *On a deserted city street, a mugger forces you to defend your wallet and your honor. What do you do?*

 a) Grasp the man in a bear hug and tell him "Thank you. I've never felt so in touch with my lower intestine."

 b) Kick up your heels and tap dance down the street. The mugger will be stupefied, especially if he's an Astaire fan.

 c) Ask the mugger to tell you what he's feeling. When he stops to think, knee him in the groin and scram.

3. *Which or whom of the following would you most like to have in bed with you?*

 a) Your devoted, loving wife of many years.

 b) A beautiful stranger whose name you're not sure of and who calls you "Slugger."

c) Sandy Duncan.
d) *Dombey and Son.*
e) The remote control of your television.

4. *If you were let loose in a sporting goods store for ten minutes and anything you could carry out was yours for free, in which department would you start?* (Essay Question)

5. *Which of the following most accurately describes your life goals?*
a) A girl who's three feet tall with a flat head.
b) Oneness with a loving partner who's caring, open, honest, and three feet tall with a flat head.
c) Tight abdominals, loose collar, and a warm place to sweat.
d) A toupee that fits.
e) To avoid rush hour traffic by any means necessary.
f) None of the above. My goals in life are (Short answer): _____

Put down your pencils now. Close your books now.

That wasn't so bad, was it?
Well, anyway, it's over. Now we can roll up our sleeves and get to work.

PART II

..

Twelve Steps to Man hood

WARNING

••

Renovating a crumbling manhood takes more than plasterboard and a coat of paint. Your soul has suffered a terrible loss. Before you can recoup it, you must mourn. The process begins with sulking, then progresses to sniveling and feeling sorry for yourself. Next comes acknowledgement: the recognition that there is a Higher Power, and that's who screwed you up in the first place. Rail at the Higher Power for awhile. Soon you'll be complaining, wailing, grumbling, and bitching at everyone, finally lamenting and whining so much you antagonize them. This is good because then *you know you're really reaching out.*

When you touch others with your misery, you make them see you as a whole man, seeking the things a whole man needs at work, at play, from your family, from your lawn furniture, from total strangers. Should they choose to cross the street when they see you coming as a result of your self-improvement, so be it. I like you anyway, and so do many others, including your mommy, probably.

Remember, centuries of indoctrination have led you to believe that spiritual and emotional starvation are normal for men, like the loss of your baby teeth or fontanel, the soft spot on top of an infant's head. It isn't. I mourn for my baby teeth and fontanel too, but I've been at this a long, long time. First things first.

The twelve-step program is based on *Fire in the John* as best we can decipher it (*see Appendix*). The appropriate fragment of the text and a brief analysis preface each step. The steps deal with all significant areas of male experience: the first four with work, the second four with mating, the final four with settling down to raise a family and, in due course, die.

Why begin with work? Freud would say the proper starting point from which to rebuild a life is the bedroom. But consider: This is the judgment of a man who puffed huge phallic cigars until his jaw fell off. Do you trust him?

No matter how important or rewarding your job is, finding a new one is easier and cheaper than divorce, especially if you factor in relocation, alimony, and child support.

As consolation during the trying times ahead, I offer the following prayer. Memorize or at least carry it with you on a piece of paper. Use India ink so it won't run should you need to consult it in your sweat lodge. Some men have the words tattooed on their bodies. This may seem an extravagant and unsanitary gesture of dubious ritual significance, but depending on where it's located, a tattoo is a surefire way to break the ice at parties.

THE MAN'S PRAYER

God (or other divinely abled, incorporeal, supreme being or being-equivalent), grant me the strength to lift large bags of groceries into the trunk of my car without rupture (especially if anyone I know is watching), the finesse to get my hibachi going without callously polluting the atmosphere with buckets of starter fluid, and the wisdom never to venture into the light of day with my fly unzipped.

TOTE THAT BARGE: WORK

••

Don't Take it Anymore—Share it!

Then Hans go back to the house,
Hear [the] WOEman crying,
Tell me that I'm lyin', ['bout]
A job . . . that I never could [indecipherable] . . .
Sa-na-na-na-na-na-na-na-na . . .

Fire in the John, *fragment 1*

ANALYSIS: The boy experiences difficulty with work, and reports back to a woman who is important to him ("the WOEman," not just "a woman"). Freely expressing her displeasure, she cries while the boy lapses into rhythmic, chantlike doggerel, not unlike drumming. He feels unjustly accused but is unable to articulate his objections. There is no man around with whom he can share his distress, not that he's in any shape to share anything. His career difficulties have rendered him irrational.

Speechlessness is next to manliness. It is widely acknowledged that most men cannot talk about anything with other men besides cars, sports, and Madonna. If not actual subjects of discussion, they are the metaphors for everything else:

MAN #1: I've won the lottery! I'm rich! I'm rich!

MAN #2: Home run. Hole in one. Swish. You win big. Get yourself a material girl and party hearty, man!

MAN #1: Fuckin' A.

Of all the taboos imposed on male intimacy, the most stringent is the one against emotional displays of any sort:

MAN #1: I've won the lottery! I'm rich! I'm rich!

MAN #2: What great news! Put 'er there (SHAKES HAND, CLAPS MAN #1 ON BACK).

MAN #1: (RECOILING) What are you, some kind of fruit?

When a man wants to reveal deep emotion, he seldom uses speech. He resorts to other forms of expression, such as the hives you get at the sight of your boss or the stutter you develop on third dates. There are other alternatives: We may curse, eat lots of pretzels, or whistle Sondheim tunes off-key in crowded elevators. Manly tradition binds us to a code of restraint, but it cannot make us altogether docile:

FIREMAN (BREAKING DOWN DOOR): The building is on fire! Everybody out!

MAN: Yo. In a minute.

The problem is not simply a male one. Our society discourages serious communication in general:

FIREMAN (BREAKING DOWN DOOR): The building is on fire, lady! Everybody out!

WOMAN: My nail polish is still wet. Shouldn't a gentleman knock before entering?

FIREMAN: Jesus Christ, lady, scram!

WOMAN: Language! I'm Lutheran.

SPEAK SOFTLY . . .

Speaking freely is risky. The best Hans can do is mumble. A growing number of men are using creative mumbling as a stepping-stone to honest communication:

CLIENT: It's a pleasure to meet you. I know we'll enjoy working together.

YOU: (SHAKING HAND) I'm sure we will. (MUTTERING UNDER BREATH) Stupid dip.

CLIENT: What did you say?

YOU: I said you've got a hell of a grip.

This isn't really honest expression, as successful mumbling eludes comprehension by anyone within earshot. But it provides the speaker with an experience of saying what he means, even if nobody else knows it. It's a start.

. . . AND CARRY A BIG SHTIK

Others find humor a useful tool. A man whose Trickster is well developed enjoys an advantage other men do not. Everybody loves a funny man. Shakespeare's fools always tell the truth and get away with it. How can you dislike a guy with the guts to walk around in harlequin tights? Even in a business suit you can say the unpardonable if you do so facetiously:

BOSS: I'm off to the shareholder's meeting. How do I look?
YOU: You look fine, Gorgonzola-breath.
BOSS: Ha, ha, ha. Guess I forgot to brush my teeth.
YOU: No problem, amigo, just stay upwind.

FROM TINY ACORNS

With the euphoria of self-discovery that many men gain when they embark on this program, you may feel ready for more honesty than others can bear. Don't plunge prematurely into frank revelations even if you think you're up to it. You will scare those less frank than you into avoiding the water cooler whenever you approach.

Instead, start small. Break up the daily run of innocuous chitchat with tiny moments of truth. It doesn't have to be earthshaking to be honest. You can be honest about the weather:

COLLEAGUE: It's raining.
YOU: It always rains when I wear new shoes. When I was a kid my mother made me wear galoshes to school over new shoes. Even if it wasn't raining. (SIGH) All the other kids laughed. (SNIFFLE)
COLLEAGUE: Oh. I have to go now.

You can be honest about clothing:

COLLEAGUE: Nice tie.
YOU: I hate ties. I hate the way they feel: tight,

binding around my neck. I'd loosen the knot, but everybody looks at you funny if you do that around here. They're a ripoff, too. They cost a fortune and you can't clean them without ruining them. Every time I wear one I like, I spill soup on it. And did you ever notice where they point? Down There, usually.

COLLEAGUE: Oh. I have to go now.

ESCALATION

As confidence develops you can extend the terms of your honesty. Tell people what you really think about the life of the office. You will become known as someone who can be relied on for an honest opinion:

COLLEAGUE: Have you heard? My brother Bob's been promoted.

YOU: That idiot? He doesn't have the brains God gave industrial carpet.

COLLEAGUE: Oh. I have to go now.

Don't just blab your opinions all over the place. Make sure you're confiding in someone worthy of your candor. Trusting the wrong man can be harmful:

YOU: I'm not bitter or anything, I just think one of us should've been promoted.

COLLEAGUE: Actually, I have been. I'm Bob's boss.

YOU: You've been promoted? No offense, but you're even stupider than Bob. What a pair you'll make.

COLLEAGUE: Oh. You have to go now.

Whom Do You Trust?

The competitive atmosphere of the workplace makes it difficult to find soul mates among the men you work with. While there are no incontestable methods to flush kindred spirits out of the corporate woodwork, careful attention to the messages you hear on answering machines is sure to tell you something about their owners:

Soft Male Phone Message: Hello, you've reached 999–9191. As any fool can tell, I can't come to the phone right now. I'm either working too hard or drinking too much. My secretary isn't around either. Who knows where that bimbo is? Anyway, leave a message and I'll get back to you as soon as you feel really insignificant and ready to give up ever hearing from me. Wait for the beep, dope.

New Man's Phone Message: Greetings, omshanti, shalom, hi—whatever. No one's here or else something is going on that's just too beautiful to interrupt with a phone call. But don't take it personally. In fact, don't take anything. Joke! Instead, leave me a message including your name, sign, and a little something about yourself. Surprise me. I'll get back to you as soon as me and my telephonic persona are in harmony. Th-th-th-that's all, folks.

Your New Place in the Office

As word spreads among your peers of your new forthrightness, they will treat you differently. Whereas once you slipped into your workstation unobtrusively, now you may find totems and talismans greeting you as

The New Man's workplace moments after he's arrived.

tribute when you arrive: small dolls decorated with pins, crumpled papers set ablaze, dead fish, or chickens. Your desk will become a sacred or ritual space within the world of your workplace. When you are there, others will approach you carefully or not at all. Your colleagues may move their desks across the room or even to another floor out of deference to your spiritual purity. Your journey has begun. Now if only you could get the chicken feathers out of your filing cabinet.

STEP TWO
UPMANSHIP VIA DOWNMANSHIP—
COMBAT IN THE COMPETITIVE ZONE

Is he serious or is [he] playin',
Papa-oo mow mow is all he's sayin',
Papa-oo. Papa-papa-papa-ooo . . .
Fire in the John, *Fragment 2*

ANALYSIS: The boy in our story is puzzled by a man he meets. He understands the man's ranting, simple cries for the Lost Father, the preoccupied parent whom countless men remember only as a disagreeable lout surgically affixed to a beer can. What puzzles the boy is the speaker's attitude. Are the cries frolicsome or mournful? Is he serious or is he playin[g]?

No matter. The man has unsettled the boy. He has won. But what has he won? If only we had more of the text. But what is there is clear enough: Empty competition reawakens the memory of the father and with it, the desire for the old fool to say something other than papa-papa-papa-ooo.

A Very Personal Cry of the Heart
From the Author

If I've said it once I've said it a thousand times, to men of all shapes and sizes, in sweat lodges and tepees, in Masonic temples, and at backyard barbecues, wherever gatherings of men raise enough to pay my lecture fee. Do they listen? I suppose. Do they hear? That's anybody's guess, but here goes for one more time:

You will never be half the man you could be, and neither will those lily-livered, torpid jerks you work with, until you all get together and CONSCIOUSLY REJECT THE IDEA THAT YOU ARE ALL IN COMPETITION! Once you have beaten it into your thick skulls that EVERYTHING IN LIFE IS NOT A CONTEST, you'll finally be ready to REALLY KICK SOME BUTT! Butt that will stay KICKED. Do I make myself CLEAR?

Of course, I'm not speaking of competitive blood lust here, only wholesome aggression. There's a difference. The possibilities for defusing competitiveness at work are innumerable:

• Interrupt a sales meeting by suggesting that everybody unwind with breathing exercises. Volunteer to lead them.

• Hide the copy toner during lunch on Friday so everybody can get an early start on the weekend.

• Wear your joke lobster Bermudas to the company picnic. Drink so much beer you barf in someone's golf bag.

The New Man's campaign need not be as costly as you may fear. Many of us have rebounded from professional disaster and successfully retrained. Some have done so several times.

THE PERVERTED WARRIOR

Competition is a degraded, polluted by-product of the Warrior energy that once informed our actions. Men live with the genetically encoded feeling that at any moment they may have to fight to the death to protect the settlement.

This genetic information had a lot more value to the organism back when our forebears might have actually had to fight to the death to protect the settlement. Nowadays we have smart bombs and a volunteer army complete with girls. Did I tell you they even let'em fly jets now? It's unlikely you'll be called up to active duty while you're on your way to the office. Especially at your age.

We know this. We know that no army in this nation's history has ever been made up of men whisked off the street and marched to the front while still in their wingtips. But the anticipation remains. And the pain.

Even though we have no outlet for our morbid expectations, they must be acknowledged so we can deal with them. The New Man believes that every man is a veteran and as such is entitled to benefits under the GI bill.

The effective Warrior is the Warrior that has a King to follow, to give focus to the need for aggression. Abraham Lincoln, Winston Churchill, and Henry IV Part One were true Kings.

Our times do not hinge on great kings or the importation of spices from the Orient: the timeless things that really matter. So man's aggression turns to the nearest King on hand. Today's Inner Warrior fights for the good of the firm. His king is usually somebody shortish and stocky in a suit, like Lee Iacocca, who says things like "bottom line," and "from day one."

The Inner Warrior is no dope, however, and will make you grind your teeth at night and experience heartburn after we spend too much time sucking up to these bargain-basement kings. Sometimes the symptoms are worse. Fortunately, today's successful Inner Warrior usually has access to a sound medical plan.

Fire in the John

WOMEN AT WORK

You can work out a lot of your feelings with women on the job unless you've been foolish enough to become Emotionally Involved there. If you are, may I be the twelve thousandth to say, *"What the hell do you think you're doing?"* Even a New Man knows that you don't dip your pen in the company ink.

The New Man respects the New Woman for her

This unsung New Man rises to the challenge of baldness with self-acceptance and Turtle Wax. Afraid to feel? Who loves you, baby?

achievements even if they were attained at the expense of an indefinable *Je ne sais quoi*. He treats her with the respect due an equal, but with a keen sense of his own maleness. For this reason he decorates his wastepaper basket with a tiny basketball hoop at which he invites her to try her skill whenever she passes by. He is an ardent fan of all the local teams and assumes all the women he works with are, too.

But he is more than cheerleader for a bunch of franchises: He is part of a team. When he sees a female colleague flagging in pursuit of a team goal, he is not above playful teasing or taking her aside for an intense talk. He may even dispense a few brisk slaps across the face—followed, of course, by a restorative hug. He eschews condescension. He can be himself. He is with a woman he does not have to make like him.

All this changes when the New Man has a female boss.

WORKING FOR THE (WO)MAN

Totally impartial research shows that the vast majority of executive women are desperately unhappy, whether or not they know it. Who knows why? Could it be they're too damn bright for their own good? No less an authority than Air Chief Marshal Kaset Rojananil points out, "Intelligent women tend not to be good-looking." This is the man who recruits stewardesses for Thai Airways, so he should know.

I prefer the mythopoeic explanation. The female boss has a seriously enlarged Inner Warrior. It's all swollen and puffy, like an inflamed tonsil. She should take a couple of aspirin and get off her feet, but will she listen? Ha.

In recognition of the executive woman's pain, the New Man does nothing to exacerbate her keen sense of inadequacy. Above all he avoids all forms of sexist language, or indeed any turns of phrase that a woman might find demeaning. He might, for example, say:

"Hey, babycakes, how's about rustling me up some paper clips?"

But he would never, under any circumstance, say:

"Hey, babycakes, how's about rustling me up some paper clip*ettes?*"

As you slowly break the pattern of competition-dependence a new world opens to you. It is a world you know little about because no one has ever shown it to you. You need a teacher.

STEP THREE
TAKE ME TO MY LEADER—
FINDING A MALE MENTOR

I will follow you,
Follow you wherever you may [go,]
There isn't an ocean too ydeepe,
Or a mountayne so high it can keep,
Keep me away . . .

Fire in the John, *Fragment 93*

ANALYSIS: Our hero has evidently latched onto someone he prizes dearly and he declares his determination
to stick by that person regardless of the other's efforts to
get away. We assume that person is male, since what
woman in her right mind would set out across oceans
and mountains without packing so much as a lunch box
or a change of clothes? No lunch box is mentioned in
the text. The object of the boy's devotion is the mentor
all men need.

Why a Mentor?

Men must learn about maleness from older men. They
cannot learn from books, their peers, or even from
experience. This may sound like men are so pig stupid
it's a wonder they don't all drown from looking up when
it rains, but it really just shows the importance of
tradition and ritual in the transmission of knowledge.

The male mentor is a nurturer. He has mastered his
Inner Feminine, but that doesn't mean he's necessarily
going to share it with you, unless you offer to share
something in return, say your hot curlers. A good male
nurturer is hard to find, despite the fact that most
successful CEOs and managers are considered "real

mothers" by their underlings and a surprising percent-age like to wear women's underwear.

OH DAD, POOR DAD

We recall the companionship prehistoric fathers and sons enjoyed. Without sons, fathers would have had no one to boss around when the women were down by the river bank, whomping laundry against boulders. From their dads, boys learned to sort flints into axe grade, knife grade, and Zippo lighter grade. Gradually, they learned more complex skills, like converting sticks and random garbage into crystal radio sets in the timeless quest to get some box scores. And it was the fathers who

Stone Age soul mates: the Venus of Willendorf and the Penis of Willendorf.

passed on the wisdom of their own fathers, wisdom such as "No matter how much you squirm and you squeeze, the last drop goes in your B.V.D.'s."

The nurturing aspect of fatherhood is neglected in our society, where fathers are usually gone for the day before their children have decided whether they want canned or fresh fruit on their cereal. But the male nurturer is seen in fetishes and pictograms dating back to earliest times.

Since the modern father is too busy to nurture his son, boys learn to be men from their mothers. And what do they know about flints? How many Moms know how to throw a slider? It's no wonder so many men today don't even know how to squirm and squeeze. No one is teaching them.

SELECTING YOUR MENTOR

Not all old men are cut out to be mentors. Walk up to the first doddering gent you see, ask him to teach you what he knows, and you're liable to get a long lecture on avoiding gluten. Watch for the telltale signs of someone who's been around the block and has something to pass along besides a kidney stone:

•A man with a key to the executive washroom is someone who's got his priorities straight and has the rewards to prove it. Stick with him and he may let you copy the key.

•A man who drinks brown liquor rather than spritzers or vodka tonics is someone you can trust. Amaretto and Kahlúa do not count. A taste for whiskey without ice and just a splash of water to bring out the nose is the most auspicious indicator of mentor potential, beverage-wise.

Fire in the John

The N.F.L. employs mentors during pre-season. Here Joe Montana's mentor demonstrates the forward pass seconds before equally geriatric front line demonstrates the sack.

•Observe senior members of staff during meetings. Those who drift off have enough on their plates without taking on a disciple. Those who aggressively warm to the cut and thrust of discussion while eyeballs roll and partners slouch are still trying to prove themselves. You want the gent who looks bored but alert, above the fray, maybe even beyond the fray, but not frayed.

APPROACHING YOUR MENTOR

Not every older man who could be your mentor will want to be. He may have novitiates already, or grandchildren, or plans to retire and take to the road in an RV, in which case it's probably just as well not to get involved. Equally likely, though, is the possibility that you will scare off your quarry by presuming too much.

As a man in search of guidance, you want to look

open and questing, but not needy. Physical contact is to be avoided at all costs, unless the man has a stroke while you're standing next to him or you've already formed the mentor bond (see *Hugging like a Hetero*, p. 136). Here is an unsuccessful mentor bid:

YOUNG MAN: I think I'll have one foot in the grave by the time I get promoted around here. Whoops, no offense. Here, let me help you with that.

OLD MAN: Take your hand off my pen.

YOUNG MAN: Sorry, I was just trying to prevent you from—see? The ink is staining your pocket. Let me take it for a moment, I'll wipe the ink off it. My fingers are already smudged. Here, I'll just—Oops.

OLD MAN: You've stained my tie.

YOUNG MAN: Who cares, right? It's only money. By the time I'm your age, I hope I'll be above such things, right? Who wants to sweat the small stuff? I'd love to get together with you and talk more about this some time. How about it?

OLD MAN: Fine. I've got to go now.

By way of contrast, here another young man makes successful contact:

YOUNG MAN: Excuse me, could you help me turn on my computer?

OLD MAN: Try the button that says "On-Off."

YOUNG MAN: By god, it worked. How did you know that?

OLD MAN: Trial and error.

YOUNG MAN: Experience counts, doesn't it?

OLD MAN: I suppose so.

Fire in the John

YOUNG MAN: I've always been bad at mechanical things. My shop teacher used to say I wasn't worth the powder it would take to blow me to Jericho.

OLD MAN: That's what my shop teacher used to tell me too. Where'd you go to school?

YOUNG MAN: You mean you weren't always gifted with your hands? The way you knew how to turn on this thing. What authority!

OLD MAN: Nothing to it.

YOUNG MAN: If you've got a minute, I've got this knot in my shoelace.

Unemployed mentors hoping for the best outside Bill Moyer's office.

Before long, mentor and surrogate son will be spending hours together, older telling younger of his army days, the collapse of his marriages and his personal resuscitation thanks to the ministrations of Miss Cataranzano in Accounting, and so on. The renewal of his manhood has gone almost as far as it can in the workplace. Only one step remains.

STEP FOUR
WE SEE BY OUR OUTFITS
THAT WE ARE BOTH COWBOYS—
INITIATION

Get right down to the real nitty-gritty,
One, two . . . the nitty-gritty,
Double beatin', keep repeatin'
Get right down to the real nitty-gritty,
Yeah! [indecipherable] . . .
Fire in the John, Fragment 15

ANALYSIS: The boy is taking or giving orders to repeat a pattern of steps or words. It is a ritual. He celebrates its successful completion with an exultant, "Yeah!" His status has changed. He has been initiated, but into what?

Why Should a Grown Man Get Initiated?

Anyone who's ever eaten lunch at a men's club knows that the food is more a test of loyalty than privilege of membership. Men do not dutifully chomp wads of luke-warm roast beef hash and browning lettuce wedges because they like them. They do it to belong.

Although many men share the same concerns, they cannot appreciate their commonality without being formally initiated into it. Such rituals usually involve extensive repetition, further proof, if any is needed, that man does not learn anything the first time he hears it, as I've been telling you and telling you, hoping it will sink in.

Primitive initiation rituals celebrate puberty, often with mutilations and body decorations. Sound like fun?

Well, after thousands of years of human cultural achievement, our initiation rituals have changed. Adolescent boys are likely to celebrate their manhood at the local mall, while fraternity pledges carve paddles and streak through snow drifts in order to learn the secret handshake.

Since this book is intended for the mid-life soft male, you are probably too late to catch these particular boats. Unless you have an appetite for tattoos, circumcision, or beanies, you're not missing much. But even the civilized adult male needs a formal rite of passage to mark his next level of manhood.

His problem is choosing what to celebrate, now that puberty is a dim memory. With help, he'll find something.

SECRETS OF THE MENTORS

The possibilities for midlife initiation are endless, but they all begin with the teaching of the mentor. Depending on his dedication and range of knowledge, your mentor can teach you:

• When to pick up the check and when to suggest you go dutch.

• How many hawk feathers should go in your headdress.

• Sound tips on municipal bonds.

• How to carve a leg of lamb. (If your mentor can teach you this, hang onto him and treat him, as the Italians say, *con molto respetto*. Such men are rare.)

• Knot-tying. Too few men know enough about knot-tying. The Age of Velcro has not made us more dexterous. Do you know how to tie a clove hitch?

Former members of the Reagan Cabinet prepare for Aboriginal theme party at the Bohemian Grove.

• To mix up your own herbal remedies.

• Hoist a jack, lay a track, pick and shovel, too, lord, lord.

• To remember to pay the phone bill.

• To call your mother once in a while. Would it hurt?

One of the advantages of recovering manhood late in life is that your initiation ritual can be a very personal matter. You can tailor it to your own specifications. You may wear a lapel pin or a fez. You could wear a sign around your neck that says MAN or a sleeve garter that glows in the dark. You may pierce your nose. I dare you.

There are subtler ways of declaring manhood. You could socialize with like-minded men in restricted enclaves. Take a trip to Bohemian Grove, the rustic, all-male California retreat favored by high government officials and captains of industry. There, you might find yourself peeing against the same tree as Henry Kissinger. Let him choose his spot. These big shots are not above making you jump back by jiggling the stream.

Whatever the badge of your particular initiation you will surely wear it proudly. For now you are ready to go forth from your mentor's side and move on to your own very special manhood. You are ready to awaken your Inner Lover. He can wake up the whole neighborhood.

DANCES WITH VULVAS: SEX

••

STEP FIVE
SOME ENCHANTED FUN RUN

[?] shake my nerves . . . [?] rattle my brain.
Too much [?] drives a man insane.
[?] broke my will, but what a thrill.
Goodness gracious! . . . Greate balls of fyre.
Fire in the John, *Fragment 219*

ANALYSIS: Hans is ready for something. It may not be marriage, but he is rocked by strong passions. He refers to feeling heat in his belly—lower, actually. This man wants company.

We marry late nowadays, when we marry at all. In tribal cultures, marriage follows so rapidly on the tails of weaning, puberty, and initiation that the average poor slob has a lean-to full of mouths to feed by the time he's noticed his voice has dropped. The arrangement is the most secure way to insure the survival of the species. The sooner the young marry and settle down, the sooner they produce children.

It's different today. Many men at mid-life are divorced, unused to being single. Others have never married. Manhood doesn't always lead to marriage and marriage is no guarantee of children anymore. No one's sure our species deserves to survive in a world it's put so out of joint. It's a kinder, gentler world for snail darters but no one else I can think of. Who can think about dating in times like these?

And yet man must. The Inner Lover demands it.

Stepping Out

Asking for a date is a lost art. It begins with the youth. Teenagers don't date anymore. They loiter together in heterogeneous bands. Couples break off from the mass as desire forms a bond more powerful than the need to appear blasé.

The same approach is possible for adults, but only if you're willing to spend untold hours in art galleries and hardware stores hoping date prospects will saunter by. Then you can bump into them and start a conversation. It's a high-risk approach with little chance of success.

Love takes time. "Jane and I didn't work out. I needed someone more grounded" says Tarzan, seen at right with Ms. Right.

Improve your chances by learning to talk to women on the telephone. Many recovering soft men try to date the switchboard operators for catalogue companies and movie clock services. The latter are frequently prerecorded. This rules a measure of spontaneity out of the exchange, as well as the possibility she'll say yes, but such ploys should not be scoffed at by the truly timid man. Practice makes perfect.

Man's fear of dating is heightened by the demands of postfeminist women. Although it has traditionally been the man's place to pay the tab and hold the door open, it has also been his prerogative, if all went well, to round third and head for home. It is only recently that women have begun to object to the traditional mythic equation of woman to baseball game. Who knows why? Why they should object to a spontaneous expression of the male spirit is unclear and certainly not justified, but there it is. We must respect the aspirations of today's independent, competent, capable, mutually respectful woman, especially if we expect ever to get laid.

WHAT TO SAY

There are many ways to ask for a date. Of course, the choices narrow right down if you can't bring yourself to utter a word. Marlon Brando handles the problem best in *On the Waterfront* when he asks Eva-Marie Saint to go dancing. "Wanna spin?" he slurs in a voice so garbled you can only understand it if you slow the film down. Not all of us are such good mumblers. We need something to *say*:

•Saturday night. Eight thirty. When half the world

will be saying, "You look lovely," to the other half.

- "How's about a long walk?"
- "We'll cook. Do you like pasta?" [AUTHOR'S NOTE: All women like pasta.]
- "I only ask people with whom I really feel comfortable this question: 'Wanna mud-wrestle?'"
- "I appreciate what you're saying. We should continue this sometime."
- "You're looking damned irresistible in this moonlight, Amanda. There isn't a part of you I don't know, remember, . . . and want."

Don't be afraid to make up your own. Sooner or later some woman is going to go out with you, and you can start thinking about a whole evening's worth of dialogue. I know you can do it.

Politically Correct Mating Rituals

Today's date is more than a prelude to seduction or marriage. It should be something that both parties enjoy. It is intended to be a "shared experience." Sharing means convincing your date that what you want is what she wants. It isn't easy. There are many ways for dates to go wrong. They can be fun but unintentionally demeaning. They can be too revealing and show that you have "no chemistry." It's no wonder they're hard to plan.

Here are some activities you and your date can share that do not debase either gender:

- Take a walk on a moonlit beach. Police it for soda bottles and medical waste as you go. A romantic setting for a mutual display of good citizenship.

The New Man relishes the primordial thrill of cooking over an open fire.

• Go folk dancing. You'll both hate it, but she'll think you're a good sport.

• Turnabout is fair play. You went dancing, now you can try a sports event, but not something too violent or male dominated, say some nice fencing or women's volleyball, or a synchronized swimming exhibition. Later, not too much later with any luck, you can race-walk each other to the parking lot.

• Vow not to fight over checks. Volunteer your pocket calculator. (Your date can supply the battery should she desire.).

• Go dancing again. In spite of the fact that you hate it, act like a good sport, at least until your back starts acting up.

- Agree to take dance lessons if she will learn to hit fungoes.
- Swap tales of the wild experiences you used to have before you started taking care of yourself . . .

zzzzzzzzzzzzzzzzzzzzzzzz

OFF-LIMITS

The new man must be mindful of his own limits. You owe it to yourself and to your companion to let her know what subjects are out of bounds. All men are touchy about one subject: their driving.

Our research shows that most men would rather be considered bad lovers than bad drivers. This primordial need is particularly strong in men who drive stick shifts, which they do for reasons that have nothing to do with control on slick surfaces or better mileage. Unless it presents a clear and present danger, a man's driving must not be criticized inside the dating arena. Remember that, ladies!

LIFELINE TO LIBERTY

As your Inner Lover awakens, dimly remembered urges will revisit you. Lust of course, but also other feelings: the desire to reveal one's heart, to set up shop together, perhaps raise a family. It is then that the New Man will resort to the Sword of Indecision. He will tell his woman, "I'm not sure if I'm ready."

Great balls of fire.

The nyte we met Iye knew Iye needed you so
And if we met I'd never let you go . . .
Be . . . my . . . [be my?] . . . be my little [baby?] . . .
Fire in the John, Fragment 967

ANALYSIS: Our hero has had quite a night. Now the companion he lusted after (see Fragment 219, p. 93) is someone he must have. If he can, he will never release her. What has happened to him? Has his soul opened to the bright light of another's love? Or is he the victim of a cruel ruse?

Romantic Semantics

Despite enormous changes in the psychosexual landscape some principles remain unchanged. The language of love and courtship mean fundamentally different things to the male and female of the species. Especially now, when man is so out of touch with his Inner Lover he frequently forgets he has one at all, leaving his date's Inner Lover without an escort.

Women are not only more in touch with their Inner Lovers, they touch base every so often with their Inner Caterers and Inner Planning Committees. Then they sneak a peak at their biological clocks. A woman's psyche is a busy place, so it's best to call first to make an appointment.

Misunderstanding between the sexes is inevitable. You may present your love with a small ring, a token both of your esteem for her and your respect for the mineral world; she thinks you've gotten engaged. Short of hiring a third party to translate for you, which can be embarrassing in confined situations such as bed, there is little we can do to overcome this language barrier.

Here are some further typical male-female misunderstandings:

YOU SAY: What would you like to do tonight? See a movie? Eat out? Or stay home, order in, and veg out in front of the tube?

SHE ASSUMES: He wants me to choose what I would like to do tonight.

YOU MEAN: Anything you want so long as it involves mushrooms, anchovies, and the listings.

•

YOU SAY: I love you. But more than that, I like you. I really like you. Know what I mean?

SHE ASSUMES: He loves me and he likes me.

YOU MEAN: I have to go now.

HOMOSEXUAL TENDENCIES

Some men feel little erotic energy with women but quicken around other men. This may or may not be lust. I tell them not to worry. The term "homosexual" did not come into being until the nineteenth century when the popularity of velveteen and Oscar Wilde gradually led people to the conclusion that something funny was going on, and not just in those fancy English schools. Previously the term used to describe men who were sexually drawn to other men was *that way*, as in "Don't look at me *that way*, Vince. This duck blind is crowded enough." The steps required to liberate homoerotic men from PMMS are precisely the same as that for heterosexual men, except gay men are better dancers.

As we descend deeper into middle age, the ratio of agreeable, presentable men to perfectly charming, more than desirable women decreases exponentially. Men dismissed as puerile toads in their twenties take on a new patina of attractiveness as the forties draw in, similar to a well-worn pair of slippers or a gnawed pipe stem. This phenomenon is called the Rising of the Saps.

So don't knuckle under to pressure. Think about how indecisive Hamlet was. Plenty of women like Hamlet. Remember the words of George Bernard Shaw, who said "It is a woman's business to get married as soon as possible, and a man's to keep unmarried as long as he can."

Relationships are like hungry jungle cats. Sooner or later they back you into a corner and you have to choose. Dare you get closer and pat its head to calm it down or should you make a break for it and run like hell?

It's not too late.

George Bernard Shaw (1856–1950) was very hairy and knew what he was talking about.

STEP SEVEN
WARTS AND ALL—THE ART OF SHARING

He says,
"I yknowe yew. Yew yknowe ymee."
Hold you in [my arm-] chair,
Yew can feele [hys] dis-Ease.

Fire in the John, Fragment 821

ANALYSIS: Hans is using the third person to describe his adventures. He and the beloved have exchanged enough intimacies to feel they know each other. They share a chair. But they share more: foreboding, a dark cloud, dis-Ease. Or have they just run out of conversation? Hard to know without more of the text.

The great privilege of intimacy is the opportunity to really know and be known by another. When I say know, I mean *know*. Your mate should be someone you can confess all the really embarrassing, offensive, unspeakable, despicable, unmentionable secrets that you wouldn't let on to a priest hearing your deathbed confession.

Few men are ready for such candor and not many women either. Be careful. If your woman would rather hear your All-Star picks than help you understand your need for a night-light (even during the daytime) your future as a couple is doubtful.

THE DANGLING CONVERSATION:
I hate to bring up impotence again, but many men I speak to tell me that bringing up the problem is about all

they can bring up. Ha!

Just joking. For the man in mid-significant relationship, let alone on the verge of a major spiritual breakthrough, the detumescence of Little Mr. Vim (or whatever you call it—er, him. See "Name that Tool," p. 144) can be a major letdown.

Imagine for a moment a man, let's call him You, is in bed with an Other and something is amiss Down There:

YOU: Oops. Moving right along, there must be some mistake, nothing personal, it must have been something I ate.

SHE: It's all right.

YOU: My briefs are too tight, my boxers are too loose, the weather makes everything limp, I haven't been eating my Wheaties—

SHE: It doesn't matter.

YOU: This has never happened to me before.

SHE: I've heard that before. From you.

YOU: Oh. My allergies have been acting up, it's my fear of getting involved, not that we're not already involved, but part of me is withholding itself.

SHE: I'll say. Look, forget it. No problem.

YOU: It's not you, it's all women. I respect you too much. I guess in my way I'm scared that if I can't, you know, then you might not think as much of me and that makes me angry with you, even though you haven't, because I have. I mean I'm the one that hasn't but that doesn't mean that—

SHE: *Pipe down*, would you?

We notice two things immediately: The man is a babbling wreck and the woman is lying like a rug when she says it doesn't matter. It matters to both of them, very much. Camille Piglia, the radical feminist, says that there is no case of impotence that can't be cured with exercise, diet, and what she calls "my special brand of Boogielove." She is also prepared to share the recipe for her health shake with readers of this book. She claims it is more effective than spray starch.

But impotence is more than a vast disappointment. A flaccid penis is a messenger from the Inner Lover, singing his song of loss.

Impotence is an indicator that you have not shared your despair and discontent sufficiently and now your penis is going to share it for you. Nice of it, really.

Nine Bazillion Ways to Leave Your Lover

Not every romance is meant to be. When you realize for the umpteenth—opinions vary on just how many umpteen is—that you are not Ready, Willing, or Able (or any combination thereof), it is time to bail out. Of course, this is hard to do in a way that leaves you and your erstwhile partner unscathed. Fortunately, there has been no dearth of research in the field of breaking up.

ACCEPTABLE EXCUSES FOR
BREAKING UP

- We've plateaued.
- I'm going through too many changes now.
- I'm not fit for any woman until I know who I am.
- Matrimony is a farce. It just props up the patriarchy.
- It's not you. It's all women.

UNACCEPTABLE EXCUSES FOR
BREAKING UP

- I've met someone I like better.
- You really get on my nerves.
- Your feet's too big.
- You say tomato, I say tomahto.
- Hasn't anybody ever taught you how to floss?

FAIL-SAFE

There are times when the strain of severing ties is too great for both parties. When that is the case, there is only one alternative. As you're leaving one evening, you simply say, "I'll call you tomorrow." Then you don't.

Of course, sometimes it doesn't work.

STEP EIGHT
GO TOGETHER LIKE A HORSE 'N' DACHSHUND—
GETTING HITCHED

It may start with a simple conversation,
My Darling, please put me on trial,
Inside, your heart starts [a] beating,
As each steppe drawes you closer to the Aisle.

Fire in the John, *Fragment 20*

ANALYSIS:The sinister tone we felt in the last fragment has now subsumed poor Hans. A few innocent words, a "simple conversation," have been his undoing. His proposal is a plea for judgment ("Put me on trial"). He has a vision of himself drawn down an aisle, as if toward a gallows. Is this his judgment? To be drawn down an aisle? It is inevitable, it seems, but hardly fun. "Well," Hans seems to say, "C'est la vie."

Modest Proposals

When the jig is up, stop fighting and propose. The modern woman will pretend not to care if you do this traditionally, down on your knee and begging. The modern woman lies when she says this, but don't make a scene. Just get down on that knee. What you say from the supplicant position is immaterial, providing you make it clear that you are abject with fear that she will refuse you. Put this across convincingly or doubts will fester and later, long after you're married, she will short-sheet your side of the bed and stir yogurt into your coffee instead of half-and-half. Beware of the rage of an Other unsure of your love.

ACCEPTABLE PROPOSALS

- I'm gonna put you on a pedestal so I can always see your feet.
- We should raise a family: boy for you, girl for me.
- Let's cast our lot together, and to hell with the hindmost. What is the hindmost anyway?
- Let's share our lives. You first.
- I need you to complete my personhood.

UNACCEPTABLE PROPOSALS

- I am man. You are woman. Let's fuse.
- Might as well. Ain't getting any younger.
- Do you do windows?
- It would be just like always, only with this piece of paper.
- It's got nothing to do with us, really. It's the bloodline.

THE BIG DAY AND THE GREAT DIVIDE

Big weddings have been with us as long as women have wanted to wear tulle. When well-to-do Roman couples tied the knot, the guest lists numbered in the thousands. Gladiators fought. Everyone walked around imitating English actors, a bizarre paradox of history. Even then, the ceremony started late and the food was lousy. With thousands of years to work it out, you would think man would have evolved a wedding ceremony that can be truly shared by both halves of the couple.

It will never happen, of course.

If history and experience teach us anything about

sexual dynamics, it teaches us this:

No man will ever care enough about his impending wedding to satisfy his bride-to-be. Wedding knowledge is a secondary sexual trait in women. This goes for all women, regardless of culture, sexual preference, or economic bracket.

During the weeks preceding your wedding, you will be asked opinions on subjects you never knew existed, let alone cared about. Your future wife's friends will have views, every last blessed one of them. The militant lesbian will weigh in with her choice of china pattern. The unmarried teenage mom will know whether or not the bridesmaids' shoes ought to match their bags. As the man in the picture, you haven't a chance. Smile cheerily whenever a question comes your way. It's a symbolic gesture. No one is really listening to your answer.

THE HONEYMOANERS

Whatever awaits you in your marriage, it's nice to look back on a blissful start. These first weeks are valuable time for the two of you. You can work on that impotence problem and confront the dilemma of reconciling your mutual soul-spaces. The New Man requires more than mere luxury and wasteful self-indulgence for his honeymoon. He likes his marital rituals to have some spiritual heft. You don't get that in Atlantic City or Rome or Paris or the Caribbean, those tacky vacation spots where no one takes you seriously.

Here are some suggestions for the kind of profound honeymoon experience you seek:

- Hike up to the Arctic Circle through Canada. Brrr.
- Challenge phobias; go spelunking or sky-diving.

• Spend the time in silent meditation at a Zen retreat. Be sure to bring cookies; it's a cinch they won't have any there.

• Walk the Appalachian Trail. At night, feast on freeze-dried food and tell each other ghost stories to heat up those sleeping bags. Ah, the power of myth!

• Shatter a shibboleth. Don't honeymoon at all. If it's not going to work out, then you're just getting a head start, aren't you?

ONWARD!

Congratulations! As a married man, you've made the central commitment of your life, the only family tie that you get to choose. Now your Inner Lover, tired and satiated, is ready to knock off and have a nap, sometimes not showing his face again for twenty or thirty years, until you're too old and tired to care.

Now is the time you discuss whether or not to have children. Most men approach this decision knowing one thing for certain: they're not ready. That is why so many women begin these discussions with the news that they're pregnant.

The funny thing is, no matter how much you've thought about it, planned for it, or waited for it, it's always a surprise to find out you're going to be a Dad.

LIVING IN AN INSTITUTION: MARRIAGE AND THE GRAVE

••

STEP NINE
PARENTING LITE—THE NEW DAD

I think I'll color [this] man father . . .
Fire in the John, *Fragment 201*

ANALYSIS: Our hero has found an older male to help him. He calls him a father, though there is no suggestion that he actually has found his father. Who knows if he has or not? Fatherhood itself is a suspect role, and the word "color" suggests a stain or tinge or taint. Stains can only be eradicated with water or club soda, rubbed in very carefully with the corner of a clean cloth and then allowed to dry. Will the newly chosen father be allowed the time to let his stain dry? Or will he be rushed into the harness of responsibility without even a second to glance at the paper? If only we had more of the text.

For centuries, the ability to engender offspring, preferably male ones, was the measure and duty of manhood. Virile loins indicated the rest of the organism was in working order. Today, however, many men undertake their primeval mission so late in life that their sperm have been put on waivers. Just when they are needed to come off the bench they declare free agency or retire altogether. Sometimes it is the woman who cannot conceive. These couples need help and an infinite variety of it is available.

Alternatives to natural childbirth include in vitro fertilization, GIFT, artificial insemination, surrogacy, adoption, and, for those on a budget, turkey basters. Many of these alternatives require you to masturbate on demand, which is disconcerting enough, but then you have to hand your seed over to a sullen technician who is clearly not impressed by either your volume or motility. Don't be offended. The technician is trying to minimize contact with what he assumes to be your warty palms. Old myths die hard.

A WORD TO THE WANKER: It is much easier to produce sperm in the privacy of your own home than in the medical office where your miracle procedure will take place. You are likely to have better magazines on hand, with fewer hairs between the pages. There is also less chance of interruption. You don't want some stray medical supernumerary barging in on you just when all the dancers in your erotic fantasy have arrived and the fruited Jell-O in the swimming pool has gotten viscous. Far better to do your business at home, put the jar into a plain brown paper bag and drop it off. This is the only time in your life when you will pray to have your pocket picked.

In their quest for a natural child it is important for man and wife to refrain from blaming each other for their fertility problems. So what if you feel that during all those years she was wearing a device that has turned her insides into confetti she might simply have practiced a little *restraint*? Here is a case in which the male instinct to keep your feelings to yourself is one hell of a good idea. After all, your wife may feel that her eggs are fine and the problem is your sperm, those giggling, drunken, drug-habituated clowns, stumbling around her tubes without the slightest sense of direction, dying well before they get anywhere near the egg chamber.

Avoid bitterness. Remember, what you have is not a *problem*. It is a *situation*. Repeat that the next time you have to produce a specimen and see how fast you get results.

Adoption offers the possibility of parenthood without suffering the indignities of modern science. While abandoning the hope that your gene pool will continue, you reduce the risk that someone else will have to go through life with your Uncle Ralph's nose. You may also avoid the recurring dream endured by any man whose wife is pregnant: that you will be displaced by the new arrival. What's growing in your wife's belly looks at least your size.

When the blessed event arrives, regardless of the means of getting there, you will find that fantasy is true. You *have* been displaced by the new arrival. The child is smaller than you'd feared, but what it lacks in size it makes up for in noise level.

RELEASING THE INNER FEMININE
(WITHOUT DOING ANY HOUSEWORK)
The middle-aged men I speak to today do not recollect harmonious relationships with their fathers. Their fathers were sucked away from home into the workplace.

Their mothers raised them. As these boys grew, their Inner Feminines withered and died from neglect. Now their sons will never see their fathers acting in a nurturing way so their Inner Feminines will die, too, and the whole thing is just an endless mess. It is up to the New Man to provide a model of male nurturing even if he's never actually known any himself.

Unsung New Man and saxophone great Lester Young perfectly expressed the New Dad's position on diapering: "I don't mind the waterfall but I can't stand the mustard."

Keep in mind that nurturing is manly so long as it involves walks in the park, letting the kid watch you light the grill, reading stories at bedtime, and supervising bath time every Christmas and Easter like clockwork. However, letting your child see you on all fours, feeling under the sofa for Lego pieces can cause irreparable damage.

If your wife should suggest that you might change a diaper, remember, the worst thing you can do is make a face like a prune! Instead, calmly point out that toilet training by the male parent causes flat feet. Don't stop there. Tell her that if a child sees a father doing dishes, there is a three in five chance that child will develop a stutter. This will slow your wife's momentum and you can slip away before she's rebutted your arguments.

Fire in the John

GENDER BENDERS

You can have fun with a son, but you've got to be a father to a girl. Almost everything you need to teach your son can be done through the metaphors of baseball fundamentals. Throwing, catching, getting behind your hands when picking up grounders, knowing when to slide and when to bunt—it all sounds like it means more than it means. If you can work a little hunting-gathering into the regimen, so much the better. But basically, teach the boy how to play ball and you're done. After all, it's not as if you're home that much.

Little girls are another thing altogether. They need you to make them feel safe, special, to be a model of male gentleness and strength. Buy your daughter things and fold her laundry for her. Your time with her is short; once you die, she might want to see other men. May she remember you well.

DEALING WITH AN ADOLESCENT

Margaret Mead's work in the South Pacific showed that adolescence is an invention of Western society. On the islands, the passage from child to adult is marked by a ceremony, after which the new adult must do what adults must do and no more monkey business.

Only in civilized cultures do we find a special class of individuals with the hormones of adults, the tastes of children and the credit lines of their parents. Some say this class did not come into its own until the invention of the leather jacket. Today adolescents are more than a class. They are a market segment.

Unlike advertisers, who seem to have no difficulty reaching teenagers, parents find it impossible. This is a bad state of affairs if, for example, the house is on fire and you want everyone to leave and your children haven't spoken to you or even come out of their rooms in three years. Always keep the lines of communication open with your children, even if it means knocking through a wall. But such drastic measures can be avoided if you deploy the right kind of conversational gambit in your dealings with them.

We noted earlier that the human fetus does not become fully human until approximately the age of fourteen or whenever it can identify its favorite Beatle. Today we face the possibility of fetuses who will not know who the Beatles were! What then? What will we do when all common ground between teen and parent disappears?

We'll fake it.

Hall monitor at suburban high school reflects current trends in fashion and posture.

WHY DON'T THEY UNDERSTAND YOU?
Ten Things to Say to Your Children that May Make Them Loathe You Less.

- Think I'll change the oil filter on the car. Want to help?
- If it's okay with your mother, it's okay with me.
- How much do you need?
- Metallica has some good songs.
- Of course you can have a pajama party.
- How much could you use?
- Okay, everybody, time to talk about my will.
- For all I care, you can have twelve Yodels.
- My first car didn't even have seat belts.
- If it's okay with your parole officer, it's okay with me.

YOUTH ENVY

There are thousands of reasons to be glad you're no longer a child. Unfortunately, presiding over your children will obliterate them all. True, you don't have to deal with school pressure, learning to use a toothbrush, or wearing a diaper to bed. But children have one thing going for them that you don't: They're a lot younger. And as you're slowly losing your powers, they're just coming into their own. No wonder you find yourself envying them. Watching a child grow is the surest way to feel your own mortality.

One day you will notice that your child has moved away from home, and is trying to get off the phone with you. You've done your job right. The function of parents is to make themselves superfluous to their children. If your kids are strong enough to stand on their own two feet, to go forth and make their own lives, you know you've given all you can give.

Then, like praying mantises deprived of prey, husband and wife can start in on each other.

Step Ten
Romancing a Stone—
The Stalled Marriage

Yew n'er close yer eye[s], [anymore] when I kiss your lips,
There's no tender[ness] lyke befawre in yer pfingertips.
Yawre tryying hard not to shew it, but baybee . . .
Baybee, Iye yknowe [it} . . .
Yewve lost that [lovin'] feeling . . . [whoa-oa]
That lovin' [feeling] . . .
Fire in the John, *Fragment 765*

ANALYSIS: We know our boy's problem, don't we? One
day she's telling him he hung the moon in the sky, the
next, she's complaining because he forgot to pick up her
prescription for wrinkle cream. It's happened to us all.

The Death of Romance

There is nothing like family life to take the intimacy out
of marriage. Instead of "You and me against the world,"
it's "You get the crib ready, I'll clean this mess up." Soon
the erotic glow between husband and wife dwindles to
the wattage of a luminous watch dial.

But gradually your child outgrows the need for your
full attention. Husband and wife get their lives back and
it's just you two again, only older and wearier and . . .
older. What an opportunity!

Before you decide that you can't bear to be in the
same room with each other for one more minute, take
stock. Think of all you've shared. Surely, you can
recover a little of what you once had. But how?

Institute a Dress Code

Parents of small children become unspeakably filth-encrusted and so does their home. As a father you can expect to spend long hours in need of a shave, shampoo, and clean shirt. If you are fortunate enough to have a washing machine, it will be laboring overtime to cleanse awesome piles of onesies, puddle pads, and adorable Osh-Kosh b'Gosh overalls. As the children grow, so will the amount of laundry they generate. Your own clothes will develop fungi in the corner.

This must change if you and your wife are to see each other with fresh eyes. While the parent of a three-month old may simply wipe an eggy fork on his shirt because it is the cleanest fork around, the father of a twelve-year-old should resist the temptation. (AUTHOR'S NOTE: You might try cleaning all the silverware at once sometime and putting it into a drawer so you'll know where it is. It's wacky but it works.)

At no time should hair become so greasy you can see your reflection in your spouse's bangs. And don't forget to brush your teeth once in a while!

Dating Your Wife

Plan special events to undertake together. Go someplace you both like. Act like you're going out together because you actually enjoy each other's company.

Here are some subjects to discuss: an upcoming vacation, even if you can't afford one. Pretending you can stretches the imagination. Or pick out a movie you'd both like to see and plan to go, assuming it doesn't come out in cassette before your next date, in which case you can save yourselves the trouble.

Here are some subjects to avoid: junior's toilet-training, your job, her job, junior's habit of torturing the neighbor's dog, your wife's need to lose weight, your need to exercise, who else do you know who's given up red meat, junior's problems with sharing, junior, when the guarantee on the roof expires, whether or not you can afford the repairs you need, which of you brought the money for tonight.

THE DANGLING CONV . . .

If this is still troubling you, it's time to see a doctor. What am I, a sex therapist? This is not a book for pessimists!

THE FATIGUED SPOUSE:
HOLISTIC ALTERNATIVES TO ELECTROSHOCK

A little-observed difference between men and women is the effect fatigue has on their respective sexual drives. When the husband is too tired, there is no sex. Usually, there is snoring. When the female is too tired, there is discussion. This is because there is hope. Perhaps the secret to a good sex life is in the planning:

•Reevaluate your love life. What is "an active sex life?" A volcano need only erupt once or twice in a century to be considered active. Look how impressed everyone is with Mount Pinatubo. No one calls it washed up. Perhaps you're not giving yourself a fair shake.

•Plan for more spontaneity in your leisure time. Keep some Wesson oil in the glove compartment. You never know.

•An underappreciated fact of American life is that almost everyone in the country lives within a day's drive of a large Polynesian restaurant. Polynesian restaurants have saved more couples than all the marriage counselors in the world. When you and your wife are at the end of your rope, hop in your car, drive to your nearest sweet-and-sour palace and relax.

Jewelry always works. Note necklace and smile.

A huge fruity drink in a ceramic coconut with paper parasols and pineapple chunks sticking out eases all tension. By the time you're ready to leave, you'll feel like you've had a little honeymoon, only more relaxing. Aloha!

IT ISN'T "US." IT'S YOU.

Sometimes nothing will work. No matter how hard you try, you and your wife cannot seem to work out your resentments and achieve a mutuality of concern and affection. You realize you've been pursuing all the wrong goals for all the wrong reasons and with the wrong woman to boot. But it's too late for recrimination.

There's only one thing to do: Admit your mistakes before you're inner beings catch on and really lose their composure. Awaken your dormant King and your somnolent Warrior and send them sallying forth in search of adventure. They'll go riding off dragging you behind them. It's a good time for a career shift.

Fire in the John

Step Eleven
Where Have You Gone Wrong?

If yew cn rd this yew cn gt a gd jb + mk $.
Fire in the John, Fragment 92

Analysis: Like all fairy tales, this story takes place in ritual time (Eastern Standard minus twelve hundred years, three hours and twenty minutes). The boy is now a man, and he has a vision of a new form of labor. It requires a certain measure of civilization (reading) and it promises riches. But are these riches simply financial? I think not. Everything else in this story is a symbol, why should money be any different?

The Sweat of Our Brows

In our time, we have seen the moral value of work decline. The big money is made not by tillers of the soil or teachers or healers, but by cheesy guys in suits who buy and sell things they can't even explain.

Modern man faces the need to find work that is satisfying, nonsexist, nonpolluting and still has a dental plan. It's a tall order, especially as we enter a service-oriented economy, where traditional bastions of male authority and power—such as politics, medicine, and business—are going to be taken over by women and sophisticated machinery, leaving us with new fields to conquer: mopping floors, waiting tables, and collecting welfare.

Butchery does not figure to be a growth industry as we enter the next century. The average New Man eats three grams of beef per year. High-tech farming, on the other hand, should boom, especially growing little adorable vegetables in hydroponic tanks. Unfortunately, this lucrative field will be closed to many, since man typically has a black thumb, and cannot unwrap a bunch of flowers without killing them.

Stumped? Take comfort in the fact that there are a lot of air-conditioning units out there. And someday, they'll all need to be repaired.

Retired farmer eats pipe for amusement.

If we can't redo our careers, the next best thing we can do is change their names. Even if your job involves dumping little bundles of toxic waste into unmarked barrels all around the country, you can make yourself sound like Johnny Appleseed. Today's man needs to feel that his work has some dignity:

OLD TITLE	NEW TITLE
Jack-hammer operator	Black-top vibrationist
Fortune teller	Consultant
Garbage man	Detritus monger
Plumber	Water flow shaman
Dentist	Tooth wrangler

TWILIGHT TIME

With any luck, you will eventually retire, give the finger to all your colleagues and set out with your spouse to enjoy the fruits of your sunset years.

Then you find out that the best fruit for the sunset years is compote (see *The Fruits of Your Labors*, p. 51). You don't see as well, you don't hear as well. Worst of all or best of all (you decide which), you don't really give that much of a damn. It's getting close to the end and you're still one step away from manhood.

STEP TWELVE
YOUR REVELS ARE NOW ENDED

Yew got to know when to fold 'em,
Know when to [hold] 'em,
Know when to walk away,
Know when to . . . .yuuuuugh-aaaaaah . . .
Fire in the John, *Fragment 1031*

ANALYSIS: At the end of our story, the man-boy is at peace with his world. He has found knowledge and this knowledge has informed his final decisions. Some people and things he has taken care of (hold 'em), others he has crushed with the righteous anger of a warrior in service to a true king who has taken about all the crap he's going to (fold 'em). We become men fully when we have died well. The rest is training.

Hardly seems worth it, right? In tribal cultures, the revered dead are the most honored members of the tribe. Still, death just doesn't seem like the same thrill as a ride in a convertible. While waiting for the afterlife, lord your advanced age over the rest of your family well before you start to dodder. Be long-winded, generous with anecdotes and advice. You can drag out these talking interludes in direct relation to the size of your estate. With skill and persistence, your preparations for the big D can utilize your fullest powers of manly rage, tenderness, and self-awareness-sharing-hood. There's no reason why anyone with an expectation of inheriting from you should ever forget your final years.

The Final Talking Stick

Your will is a tool. Properly used, it is a weapon. Wield it with respect, care, and grace. Alternate periods of secrecy about it with periods of endless telephoning and consultation with children, spouse, investment people. Hire an estate lawyer if one of your children offers to pay. If not, tell your children you're planning to draw up your own will, using the backs of coasters at the local tavern. If that doesn't make your children get you a lawyer, investigate: The children may be dead or, at the very least, senile.

Deliberating over you final judgments can be a fascinating, time-consuming diversion. And by skillful alteration of accusation and reward, threat and bribery, you will have come up with a project the whole family can share.

PUTTING IT ALL BEHIND YOU

Some men find in the wisdom of old age the strength to forgive old grudges, no matter how deeply held. This reflects a maturity and breadth of soul that, to me, bespeaks total spiritual bankruptcy. I know that nothing he could ever do would make me forgive the Camp Mongoose softball coach who took me off the mound in the first inning of our game against the Lizards because I threw the ball on top of the batter's cage. It was nerves. My manly rage burns to this day. Am I not entitled?

Indeed, if we learn anything through the twelve steps of this program we learn just that. We are not entitled to degrade the environment and bore the pants off each other with our crabbing and crying, but we *are* allowed to give vent to the failures and frustrations of a lifetime before we leave the stage. And it's a good thing, too.

But what's your hurry? We've got time yet. There's still a little ozone layer left. As of this writing, there are twenty-three new republics in Eastern Europe. And you've become all the man you can be without dropping dead. It's not your turn to go yet. How should you conduct yourself for the rest of your rehabilitated, manly man's life?

PART III

O, Brave New Guy

NO NEW MAN IS AN ISLAND

●●

NOW, VOYAGER

If you've stuck with the program, you're probably moist-eyed as you read this, full of feelings of timely tenderness, righteous rage and queasiness. These could be caused by the jostling of your inner beings, the bratwurst you ate for lunch, or the longing for connection with men who feel as you do. It's nothing to be ashamed of. The twelve-step program has taken you far. Still, you are not happy. You need companionship, sympathetic friends who know the path you've trodden and find it just as thrilling and challenging as you did, and still do, and always will. You need to share your grief with guys.

All over the country new men's groups are emerging. There are no golf courses or club houses. There are no dress codes; drinking is frowned upon, as are playing cards, talking sports, and embellishing tales of your conquests. (Embellishing tales of your sexual failures is not only permissible, it's the main event.) Here men come to be men, to share what they cannot share with their spouses.

One such group meets informally in my garage. We talk, we chant, we sweat and blow our noses in our hands. They are my closest, most manful friends. I would like to show them more hospitality but the little woman says our body paint stains the bolsters. Not that I'm bitter. A garage is good enough for real men. Here we talk and we talk. We discuss manly concerns such as:

- My Family: More Dysfunctional than Yours.
- Snoring: Offensive Sinus Disorder or Message from

Your Nostrils?
- •Ring Around the Collar: Who's Really to Blame?
- •My Family: More Dysfunctional Than Anyone's.
- •Masturbation: Should It Have Olympic Status?
- •Dysfunction: How Come It Has a Y?

Members of the San Luis Obispo Shaman's Cabal and Motorcycle Club demonstrate pyramidic bonding outside Bill Moyers' office. You'd think this would've caught his eye, wouldn't you?

As you can imagine, a roomful of men noncompetitively sharing their feelings can get pretty deafening. We eschew parliamentary procedure. Parliamentary rules turn men into brown-nosing creeps who'll do anything just to stand up and blather. Just look at Congress. We rely on the Talking Stick, a device used in tribal cultures to ensure that every man got his say but that no man could filibuster.

Fire in the John

As long as you're holding the sacred stick, you may not be interrupted—if you've got a quorum. If not, a simple majority of braves can vote, *even while you're speaking,* to take the stick away and paddle you until your butt is puce. So when it's your turn to hold the Talking Stick, be honest, be sincere, but get to the point.

DO THE RITE THING

Just as our society has deprived men of the ritual spaces and mentors they need to build strong psyches, so too have our public holidays been drained of any significance for men. Father's Day is nice, and you can park anywhere on Christmas, and I suppose Memorial Day celebrates mostly male heroics, but only dead males. Your men's group can fill your need to celebrate.

In our group no man's need is too small for a ceremonial observance. All one of us has to do is share the pain of paying a library fine and we spring into action. Someone holds the confessor until his tears have subsided, while someone else clears the floor. Then with a cry of "Let's put on a ritual! I'll chant, you'll drum," we're on the floor, screaming and pounding and dancing wildly. It's a lot of fun, and afterward we help clean up.

Not all rituals need be group endeavors. Here are some ceremonial possibilities that can enhance your sense of manhood anywhere at all:

•Install a hard disk in your computer by yourself.

•During the next cold snap, leave your coat unbuttoned until your thorax is numb. Feel the burn!

•Go Walkabout: Aborigines take off into the bush for months at a time when they feel the need. You can buzz off to the corner store for a quart of milk and, if your Inner Warrior is up for a little Let's Pretend, you can come home feeling renewed.

- Work out a little dance to perform as you sort your recyclables. I whistle the theme from *2001* when I knot the newspaper bundles.
- Observe a moment of silent pride every time you tape what you actually intended to tape with your VCR.
- On April 15, or whenever it is you mail in your tax return, celebrate the achievement with a cantaloupe marinated in bourbon. You get a lot of vitamins from the cantaloupe.
- Refuse Novocain at the dentist, asking instead that the dentist deal with your tears.

No ritual is complete without chanting, so we always start our meetings with a few scales and some biorhythmic breathing. There are still plenty of men for whom chanting is just childish, hippy crap. They're doing it wrong. A repeated pattern of sound with the right seismic throb will connect you to your swarthy forebears quicker than you can say "archetype." Just make sure you've got the right chant. Try one of these:

Unsung New Man Desi Arnaz introduced the healing power of "Babalu" to American audiences.

Fire in the John

CHANTS TO WAKE THE WILD MAN

1. Yee-yee-yee-yee-yee-yee-yee-yee-yee-yee, etc.
2. Yip-yip-yip-yip-yip-yip-yip-yip-yip-yip, etc.
3. Wild, wild bo-biled, banana-fana-fo-filed, fee-fi-fo-filed, Wild.
4. Oooga-chukka-ooga-chukka-ooga-chukka-ooga-chukka-ooga-chukka, etc.
5. Ooo-eee-oo-ah-ah, ting, tang, walla walla bing bang, oo-ee-oo-ah-ah, ting tang walla walla bing bang.
6. Give a yell. Give a yell.
   Give a good substantial yell.
   And when we yell we yell like hell,
   And this is what we yell.
   With a U-
   And an N-
   And an I-T-Y,
   Unity, unity, aye-aye-aye.
7. Swift as an eagle, strong as a vulture,
   Bring on back that patriarchal culture.

AUTHOR'S NOTE: Repeat any of these with rhythmic accompaniment (drums, maracas, stomping feet, etc.) until pulse quickens and you sense integration of personhood or neighbors call cops, whichever comes first.

The Sweat Lodge Experience

Many men's groups let it all hang out in small enclosures filled with hot rocks. The Indians used such structures for rituals of purification. A group of braves would enter the lodge and wait until the intense temperatures caused their pores to gape as wide as manholes. Then they rubbed each other with branches and sticks before dousing themselves with ice-cold water, closing their pores again as fast as slamming doors. Along the way, some deep, intimate discussions of skin care and personal hygiene took place. Tribal man knew the value of clean skin, even if he was covered with dirt himself.

The soot and grime of industry made on-the-job facial care a thing of the past. Ever since, the New Man has carried the pain of rough skin and blemishes. We weep for our brother's pimples even as we blush and feel deep shame for our own.

Hugging Like a Hetero

When the men of the Walibri Tribe of Central Australia visit men of other tribes, they shake penises rather than hands. I don't recommend you try this at your next men's group meeting, although who knows? Try it at Bohemian Grove and you could find yourself a Government appointee.

The Walibri aside, many men have a difficult enough time being emotional and sympathetic without worrying about sexual surprises. This is not to say that homosexuals are in any way excluded from the men's movement, any more than black, Hispanic, or working-class men. We just never see them at our meetings. In our view, they're part of the great community of males, every one of them as underprivileged, abused, and hurting as the white, educated upper-middle-class fellas who predominate in our membership, so come on down!

The man who wishes to show tenderness toward another man without creating Suspicion should proceed thus:

1) Standing at least an arm's length away from your subject, establish eye contact. Do not smile, blink, or attempt to speak; no giggling either. Now, move closer and place your hands on your companion's shoulders lightly, prepared to withdraw in the event of a shrug. Maintain eye contact until your hands are resting steadily.

Men not yet prepared to embrace compare thumb lengths instead.

2) Lean forward from the waist in the "bent fork" position (The adult version of the adolescent "gotta-

boner" stance) until face and shoulders *but nothing lower* are in contact. Move hands from shoulders and wrap around back. Pat consolingly.

3) Move hands back to subject's shoulders and push off. Re-establish eye contact and smile warmly. You've done it! And no embarrassing faux pas!

One of these men is further along the comeback trail than the other. Intimacy requires timing.

A perfect male hug. No chance of Misunderstanding.

Fire in the John

ALTERNATE ALTERNATE MEN'S CONSCIOUSNESS GROUPS

As befits our restless, probing minds, the New Men have split into factions. There are feminists, antifeminists, prolife cross-dressing lumberjacks, mythic meditators, and social activists. Here are some others:

THE MISTER ROGERS WANNABES hold a potlatch luau every year in their ritual space, Pittsburgh, home to a man who is an icon for all New Men. After all, he has never let the fact that he has the voice of a serial killer prevent him from caring more about your children than you do yourself.

The group is only open to men with prepubescent sons. Termination of membership is celebrated when Dad hangs his son's bed sheet out the window after the first nocturnal emission. The boys never forget the gesture.

Mr. Rogers greets followers outside moments before scene turns violent.

THE MEN OF K'VEST explore new dimensions in carping and general anguish-sharing. In the words of group leader Werner N'erhard, "A man is never most fully himself than when he is criticizing someone else. Would you mind not sitting there? When I'm giving another the gift of my anxiety, my rage, my depression, I know I'm alive and cooking. Did you hear what I said? Would you move, please? You're blocking my light." K'vest holds intensive weekend workshops in which participants are guided from soft, generalized whimpering to hysterical fits. There is a cramped, dark room beneath K'*vest's* drumming chamber where members take turns banging on the ceiling to complain about the noise.

THE COMMANSCHELACH interpret the Native American tribal experience for the Kosher New Man. Committed to the belief that a fellow can have a strong Inner Warrior and still be a nice boy, the group provides its members with plastic seat-covers for the sweat lodge as well as both dairy and meat tomahawks.

There are others, all grieving, all struggling, all recovering. I say the more the merrier. Given the variety and vitality of the New Men, it's a good thing we all have one thing in common: love of noise.

MEETING YOUR BEAT

It's seven P.M. in a rusting Quonset hut behind a used tire mound not far from Springfield, Massachusetts. Inside, though, it could be the Savoy Ballroom on a spring night in 1946, only without women. There are lots of men, though, crisply attired in black satin striped trousers, white dinner jackets, and brilliantined hair. On stage the seats, arranged in a perfect semicircle, catch the light reflecting off the mirrored ball slowly revolving in the center of the ceiling. It looks as if a swing dance is about to begin. Only this band consists entirely of drums. The musicians take the stage and the band leader, a ringer for Benny Goodman, taps his baton. The tapping disappears under a deafening cacophony of bass thumps, snare rolls, and miscellaneous percussive fury. It's like this every week.

THE SONS OF KRUPA share their pain within the context of the Swing Era. Members wear tuxedos and lots of Wildroot Cream Oil. Each meeting ends with a group drumroll honoring the member who most resembles Sal Mineo as he looked in *The Gene Krupa Story*. Some members know whole scenes by heart, complete with drum solos. But they are far from the only New Men who have heeded the call of skin on skin.

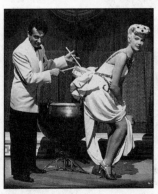

A *novitiate Son of Krupa commences his initiation.*

Drumming has its origins in pagan ritual. It takes us out of our time and space and connects us with something bigger, darker, and louder. Today, man lets everybody else make the noise. He tiptoes around when the children are asleep or just when the missus has a headache. Their grandfathers would have used either occasion to get stinking drunk and throw a lot of crockery around. And they would have been proud to do so!

Clay Vessels, Professor of Thumping at the Berklee School of Music, believes that the surge of interest in drumming is in large measure the vengeance of former clarinet, violin, and piano students. For every boy who enjoys his piano lessons, Vessels says, there are seven thousand men who'd like to chop the thing up for kindling and beat a gourd until his knuckles are raw. "What can you do with piano? Sit around at parties boring everyone with your Gilbert and Sullivan medley. Drumming connects with your pulse, the heartbeat, life itself. What can I say? Blame it on the Bossa Nova."

Budget-minded Wild Men share a drum.

TODAY I AM A NEW MAN: FURTHER STUDIES

••

There is more to spiritual renewal than just chanting when you put out the trash and getting together with your brothers once a week to bemoan and bemoan. Your New Manhood must pervade every facet of your life until peers, friends, and family alike ask you to sit down and shut up. But you won't be able to. So much that was wrong remains to be put right!

Since man first became aware of it, his organ has been nicknamed, usually by others, usually by *Them*, usually disrespectfully. Time for a change. Give yours a moniker to be proud of. Choose a name that reflects the person you really feel yourself to be. Lady Chatterly's lover named his John Thomas. You may prefer Spike or Clyde—or even Gwendolyn or Cecily. Look over the list of possibilities (see page 144).

ASLEEP AT THE VEAL

Even if you are unable to boil water at the present time, you will find that reconnecting with your Wild Man gives a fellow a man-size hunger that just can't be satisfied by your wife's cooking. Snacking can fill the hole for a while, but so many New Men tell me that their fire in the belly is just heartburn caused by junk food, I believe it's time to take the pan by the handle and learn to use it.

Remember that all the great chefs are men. Stand tall

NAME THAT TOOL

Names of Shame

cock	pud
putz	boner
salami	tube steak
dong	wee-wee
weiner	schlong
strezool	Terrible, Swift Sword
Home of the Whopper	Down There
Warren	

New Handles on the Issue

Mr. Archetype	The Secret Sharer
Bert	Ernie
Canseco	Oscar Meyer
Thelma	Moyers
Warren	

AUTHOR'S NOTE: Add to this list. You'll know the right name when you find it.

in the kitchen even if you don't know your way around. Try not to cut yourself. You probably do not yet have the nerve to wear a big white hat, so start slow and above all, remain calm. The New Man cooks as if he's been doing it all his life, so no sudden movements and no shouting, even if you mince your fingertips into your next batch of fajitas. You'll grow new ones.

The New Man prepares food that is light, healthful, and sensible. Then sometimes, when no one is watching, he washes it down with cheeseburgers and Oreo

Double Stuffs: man food. While few New Men are lucky enough to be near a source of huntable meat, nearly all of us can get on a first-name basis with the local butcher. Don't eat too much meat, it's not so good for you, but talk about it a lot. Point out choice cuts when you're shopping with your wife. Say things like "well marbled" and "dripping with juices." Your wife will be impresed, even as she whoopses into her cupped hands.

HEALTH AND FITNESS

Our distant ancestors did not have to worry about keeping fit. Just getting through the day was a workout. Our parents neglected exercise even while their world became increasingly sedentary. It became the norm for men to cease physical activity from the age of eighteen until shortly before death, when sudden outbursts of calisthenics were undertaken to make up for lost time.

The New Man recognizes the need for some program of physical activity, but he doesn't get ridiculous about it. People who suffer from tennis elbow and runner's knee are, in his view, victims of competitiveness. The New Man's need to win is slaked with less wear and tear on the organism. He cheats at jacks with his daughter or bets nickels on ball games with his son. He rides his NordicTrack against the clock and dreams of the biathlon. He likes any pastime that will allow him to justify purchases from the Patagonia catalogue, thereby creating the illusion of fitness. This is just as good as the real thing and much more restful besides.

YOU CAN TOO TELL A BOOK BY ITS COVER

The New Man is no slave to fashion. He prefers comfortably cut clothes in natural fabrics. He knows black is slimming but thinks it can be overdone. He realizes that clothing does more than preserve modesty and body warmth. He understands that clothing communicates information: about his occupation, social standing, sexual preference, and whether or not he's remembered to remove the dry cleaner's tags. These communications are the true Language of Clothes. The Soft Male doesn't believe his clothes make a sound, aside from the odd squeaky shoe or loud sport shirt. Indeed, he is so benumbed he has no idea of what he would like to wear or even what he is wearing. Listen to a friend:

"I'm a bathosphere repairman," says Elmore Fathom, not mentioning that he is also head of the Dick Divers, a men's group dedicated to underwater grieving. "My brother Delmore is a partner with Full, Fathom and Five, a very conservative Wall Street law firm. About three years ago, we picked up each other's dry-cleaning by mistake. We didn't notice and accidentally went to work in each other's clothes.

Quel surprise! The diving helmet Del wore down to Nassau Street weighs about forty pounds. I'm kind of surprised he didn't notice it right away. But he kept it on until lunch, when he wolfed a piece of sushi with such vehemence that he cracked the face plate. There's nothing like a piece of raw fish to bring out the

Delmore Fathom shows up for work improperly attired. Security guard is too polite to say anything.

Fire in the John

Wild Man in Del! As for me, I dove into 42-degree water with nothing on but a charcoal-gray chalk stripe suit with moderate waist suppression, white Oxford cloth button-down, maize foulard tie with red figures, and monk strap cordovans. Absolutely classic look of course, but it just doesn't keep the warmth in and the wet out the way my diving suit does, even with the bottom button of the vest done up. Fortunately, I realized something was wrong right away so I jumped out of the drink before the bends set in. Ruined Del's suit, though, and I still carry a lot of pain about that. Poor Del still can't bring himself to admit he ruined my helmet. Claims he wasn't even wearing it, that the sushi was bad and he hallucinated the whole thing. Poor guy is just out of touch."

The new man rejects the bland anonymity of contemporary fashion, opting for SincereWear. He likes

Stepping into the circle of the Wild Man requires proper footwear. This moccasin is cut high enough to accommodate an arch support.

jerkins, which are like vests only more ridiculous, and tweed jackets, especially the beefy kind with twigs and bits of birds' nests in them. The New Man eschews garments that come with elbow patches already in place. Elbow patches should only go on when the elbows are worn through. Anything else is cheating.

Around the house, he likes beaded moccasins and loincloths. If your loincloth is leather, be sure to have it cleaned by a professional. Feathers do well on birds, but are iffy for men, especially if you're bald and not an Indian.

STANDING ERECTILE: CONCLUSION

••

Well, guy, this is it. You've recovered from postindustrial depression and feminist slander. Your PMSS is a thing of the past. No longer do you walk around numb from the ears down, waiting for Happy Hour. You're lean, trim. You've renegotiated the contracts of all your inner archetypes and you're keeping together the infield. Even your loved ones now realize there's more to you than any of them thought they could stand.

Are you going to rest on your laurels? Ha. The New Man does not rest. He's ready to tilt with more windmills of his mind. He's learning to tie a bow-tie, he's studying T'ai Chi, he's making lanyards, he's hot-wiring the toaster so his bagel somersaults out when it's done. He's removing the shackles that have bound him to a code as destructive as it was tedious; he's bounding down to the corner store and buying all the Kleenex they've got.

It just makes me want to cry. Doesn't it make you want to cry? Let's.

Appen dix

FIRE IN THE JOHN: THE GRIMM FACTS

●●

Myths have always been valuable commodities to those who owned them. Though today regarded merely as quaint children's-book authors, in nineteenth- century Vienna Jacob and Wilhelm Grimm were folklorists with muscle. Roaming the European countryside with paper and pen ("mythopoetry in motion," their publicist claimed), their collected stories were published to acclaim. The books were best-sellers, topping lists from Silesia to Bosnia-Herzegovina. The cherry on top was the publication of *Nursery and Household Tales, Vol. II* in 1815. Offers streamed in. "Truly," Jacob wrote Wilhelm after the initial reviews broke the book big, "we seem to have fallen into a bucket of *schlag* with this baby."

The rejoicing was short-lived, however. One after another, disgruntled folk whose lore the Grimms had appropriated began showing up in Vienna demanding royalties. Many of them, it seems, had not signed releases for the use of their material. What's more, many of these anonymous "folk" were in fact professional entertainers on the provincial Austrian "hovel" circuit, playing tiny huts and outbuildings, anyplace an enterprising rustic could fit in enough other yokels to make a profit on a booking.

"I've been doing *Snow White* since those Grimm bastards were wearing three-cornered pants," complained Frau Katherina Vierhmann, "It's my bread and butter, my big finish. They promised me a chance to play Vienna. Christ, I'd play a dromedary just to perform under a roof that wasn't thatched, but it's always been my dream to play the Big Schnitzel. Now anyone can buy the book and learn *Snow White*. Everyone knows the ending. My best routine, ruined. Those two Nazis put me out of business."

The final blow to the Grimms' career was the news that they had withheld one story from publication, betraying the pledge sworn by all Viennese socio-anthropologists to share research no matter how unspeakably tedious. The story was called *Fire in the John*. When news of it leaked out, rumors flew that they had faked their folklore and that the angry peasants camped outside the Grimm family compound were actors hired by the Grimms to create a diversion from the real scandal. In truth, the story was a genuine folk myth. The Grimms did not want the world to read *Fire in the John* until it was available on magic lantern slides. They had a deal with the slide maker.

Things went downhill after the scandal broke. No publisher would touch their work now. They were dropped by their agent, Wilhelm Moritz. Eventually they made their way to America, where they found work as commercial models.

The Brothers Grimm when they ruled the folkloric roost.

The Brothers Grimm in leaner years, posing. (The real Smith Brothers had wispy beards.)

No complete manuscript of *Fire in the John* exists to-day. Poor Johann attempted to eat it in a botched suicide attempt. Only fragments remain, but what fragments they are! It's clear why the Grimms wanted to keep their hands on it. Like all great stories, it's high concept with a twist, sort of like *Days of Thunder* only more plausible. Most provocatively, in tracing the life of its hero, Hans, from childhood to death in twelve steps, it suggests that the life-force itself has a codependency problem.

SUGGESTIONS FOR FURTHER READING

•*Iron, John!* by Robert Cry (Piss and Moan Press, $19.95): Dysfunctional household tips from the Whinging Bard himself. Still not a peep about where he gets those vests, though.

•*The Feminine Mistake* by Betty Freedomland (SuppHose Books, $18.95): Hard to know what she's up to; you know how women get when they're excited. Still, at her best she offers up some hot flashes (!) of insight about how mothers try, but fathers stink. Men in general stink (What did you expect?), actually, and nothing is your fault if you're a girl. Yeah, yeah.

•*I'm Havin' My Baby* by Paul Sanka (Cojones, $18.95): A mythopoeic journey to the Neighborhood of Make-Believe.

•*Fire in the Jelly* by Sam Wean (Lymon and Cola Nut Ltd., $23.50): Spicy preserves the Cajun way, of course, and more manly tales of home-canning derring-do by Grandmaster Jam himself.

•*It Wasn't Always Soft* by Mr. Whipple (Rhino Gonad Books, $5.95): Tell-all show-biz bio by the Twittering Titan of Two-ply.

The official organ of the New Men's Movement is *Thingspan*, a quarterly dedicated to creating what editor Chris Bulging calls "the feeling of a bunch of guys sitting up late talking about their feelings, eating Tostitos, lighting farts—and coming away *enriched*." Recent articles include: "Are Whites Really Smaller? How Come?," "Bill Moyers: Trickster, Shaman, or Just Another S.O.B. Who Won't Return My Calls?," and "Come On, Whites Aren't Really Smaller, Are They?"

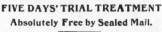

Photo Credits

p. 1: UPI/Bettmann Newsphotos; p. 3: © 1989 Barbara Rios/Photo Researchers; p. 11: The Bettmann Archive; p. 13: David M. Phillips/The Population Council/Science Source; p. 16: The Bettmann Archive; p. 24 Culver Pictures; p. 27: © Harvey Shaman/Globe Photos; p. 29: AP/Wide World Photos, © 1991 Warner Bros. Inc.; Culver Pictures; p. 31: Tom McHugh, Field Museum, Chicago/Photo Researchers; p. 34: Culver Pictures; p. 35: © 1980 Tom McHugh, Field Museum, Chicago/Photo Researchers; AP/Wide World Photos; p. 36: Laima Druskis/Photo Researchers; p. 37: AP/Wide World Photos; © Porterfield-Chickering/Photo Researchers; p. 38: Richer, Germaine. *The Devil with Claws* (Le Griffu). (1952). Bronze, 34 1/2 x 37 1/4. Collection, The Museum of Modern Art, New York. Wildenstein Foundation Fund. Photo, Art Resource; p. 40: The Bettmann Archive; p. 42: Culver Pictures; p. 44: Giraudon/Art Resource; p. 45: Reuters/Bettmann Newsphotos; AP/Wide World Photos © The Press Association, Ltd.; Charles Gatewood/The Image Works; © Renee Lynn/Photo Researchers; p. 46: Culver Pictures; p. 47: Globe Photos; p. 52: © David M. Phillips/The Population Council/Science Source; p. 55: Irving Haberman/Culver Pictures; p. 56: Reuters/Bettmann Newsphotos; p. 58: © Archivi Alinari, 1990/Art Resource; p. 65: Giraudon/Art Resource; p. 75: The Bettmann Archive; p. 79: Paul Harris/Globe Photos; p. 83: Giraudon/Art Resource (2); p. 85: UPI/Bettmann Newsphotos; p. 87: Culver Pictures p. 90: © Topham/The Image Works; p. 94: The Bettmann Archive (2);